Previously published by this author
Mr Bob

This first impression limited to 500 copies

Published by *Access Press*
P.O. Box 132, Northbridge, Western Australia

Copyright © *Robert Primrose*, 1998

Typesetting, layout and design by Access Press
Cover photograph courtesy The West Australian

National Library of Australia
Cataloguing in Publication data
On the Beat and in The Bush
ISBN 0 86445 119 9

Distributed in Australia and Overseas by the Publisher.

On the Beat
and
In The Bush

ROBERT PRIMROSE

This is an  Publication

ACKNOWLEDGEMENTS

Without the encouragement and help of my mentor, my friend Peter Good, "On the Beat and in the Bush" may not have evolved. I sincerely thank Peter for his patience and assistance in its development.

There is really nothing unique about the incidents in this book. They are the "everyday" happenings that individual policeman and policewoman deal with. I have simply sought to show how I dealt with the things I had to as a General Duties policeman, and how they affected me personally.

I am grateful to Edith Kahanguri of the St John Ambulance and Jean Hobson of the Police Library for their generous help in researching their respective historical records, enabling me to more positively identify some of the incidents I have referred to. And I thank Doreen Eaton, Nancy Lockyer, Rita Atkins, Carmel Williamson and Neville French for allowing me to use their personal photographs in my book. Also my publishers, Helen Weller and John Harper-Nelson of Access Press, who had faith in me and encouraged my writing.

I also acknowledge the encouragement and support I have again received from friends and family, particularly my wife June for being my "sounding board" and who accepted with good humour the many interruptions to our rather laid-back lifestyle during my writing.

The names of many of the people in these stories have been changed to avoid offence or embarrassment. But the incidents are factual. If any person believes they recognise him or herself and feels discomfort, I apologise for it has not been my intention to cause any.

CONTENTS

FOREWORD

I first met Bob Primrose when I visited Goomalling in 1956 in my capacity as Stipendiary Magistrate stationed at Northam. Goomalling was one of the towns on my circuit. It soon became obvious that young Bob was a very competent officer who had the respect of the local community. This competency eventually led to his promotion to Inspector and, later, Superintendent.

Since his retirement almost nine years ago he has written the book "Mister Bob", which has been published. In this, his second book "On the Beat and in the Bush", the author has given us an interesting and, at times, exciting account of his 36 years service in the Western Australian Police Force, beginning with his initial period as a probationary constable in Perth. This was followed by his appointment as second constable at Goomalling Station, where he was also involved in relieving at other country towns.

I did not meet him during the period of his service at Gwalia but he relates his experiences, which at times were dangerous , with humour and compassion in "Mister Bob". From Gwalia, Bob moved to Perth for family reasons, and served with distinction at Innaloo showing the same qualities that led to his promotion.

Bob writes very vividly and comes across as a humane, honest, tenacious and incorruptible police officer.

"On the Beat and in the Bush", as does "Mister Bob", makes gripping reading.

I have had much pleasure in writing this foreword.

Keith H. Hogg (Ret. Chief S.M.)

ABOUT THE AUTHOR

Robert Burns Primrose ("Bob") was born at Nannup Western Australia. A fourth generation Australian, his forebears on his mother's side were seafaring folk who were closely involved in the birth and development of the Swan River colony. His great great Grandfather John Watson, was an eighteen year old Royal Navy Petty Officer on H.M.S. Challenger when it arrived at the Swan River in 1829 under the command of Captain Fremantle. He returned later as a settler and in 1842 established the first boat service on the Swan River between Perth and Fremantle. His first born son Charles Henry Watson (Bob's great grandfather) was a boyhood friend of the explorer John Forrest, and as Chief Officer on the supply ship Adur, was a member of Forrest's 1870 Perth to Adelaide Expedition. Watson was also the first native born West Australian to be granted a Master Mariners Certificate of Competency by the London Board of Trade in 1876. In the I870's also, Charles Henry Watson was awarded a "Royal Humane Society Medal" for his bravery in plunging into rough seas to rescue a crew member washed overboard in a storm.

Bob however had no ambition to follow the seafaring exploits of his forebears. He joined the West Australian Police Force in 1952 at age nineteen and rose to the rank of Superintendent before retiring in April I988. At the time of his retirement he held the position of Regional Officer at Northam. Bob served more than sixteen years in the General Duties Command, "on the frontline of the Police service" as he puts it, before moving on to other specialised sections and administrative areas of the Police Force.

His first book "Mister Bob" dealt with the three year period of his service at the small goldmining town of

Gwalia. This present collection of short stories deals with the remainder of his career "On the Beat and in the Bush", as a General Duties policeman.

Since his retirement Bob and his wife spend much of the year travelling the Continent at a leisurely pace in their car and caravan.

PROLOGUE

About eight of us were crowded in the back of the first van and the remaining members of our Police Training School followed in another two police vans and an unmarked police car.

Our small convoy was travelling west in Cambridge Street Leederville on the way to our weekly motor cycle training session at Herdsmans Lake, on land behind the (then) Police Stables. As I looked forward occasionally through the rear window of the driving cab I could see Constable Ross King and Constable Derrick Woolmer two of our riding instructors on motor cycles about fifty metres in front. I knew there were another couple somewhere further ahead.

Suddenly our vehicle braked heavily and came to a stop and as we spilled from the vehicle we found that Ross had collided with a car entering Cambridge Street from his left. Derrick Woolmer, who had been riding abreast, managed to swerve to his right and avoided the car, but Ross, striking the centre of the vehicle, had been catapulted over its roof to land on the roadway beyond. He was lying where he fell crumpled like a discarded rag doll, unconscious, one arm broken, and bleeding freely from the ear and nose.

It was an eerie scene that is still indelibly etched in

my memory. There was Ross, one of our likeable instructors, lying on the road in a pool of blood – perhaps dying. I watched in awe as his fellow officer Derrick, who obviously knew him well, almost casually walked back from his parked motor cycle to bend over Ross and release his tie and shirt collar before moving him into a semi-prone position: Then having confirmed that an Ambulance had been summoned, he moved over to check the condition of the car driver (uninjured but in shock still seated in his vehicle) before unhurriedly marking the roadway where Ross lay and the rest of the crash scene with yellow crayon.

There was no sign of emotion or undue haste as this officer went about his tasks, recording details of the vehicles etc in his notebook and directing others to take over traffic control duties. Likewise when he and two other instructors had to physically restrain Ross before the Ambulance arrived, as he partially returned to consciousness and started to thrash about aggravating his injuries.

The only time Constable Woolmer's true feelings emerged was after Ross had been placed in the Ambulance. The attendant had just closed the rear door, and was moving forward to the driver's seat when the Constable clasped him on the shoulder and in a breaking voice, said "Please move as fast as you can. He's my mate"

It took a long time but Ross did eventually recover and return to work. For me as a teenage trainee policeman, what happened that day was an important learning experience: an example of the self-discipline I too must develop in the years ahead if I hoped to become an effective policeman.

Ross King with a police motorcycle – sometime before his accident.

For the men and women of the
GENERAL DUTIES COMMAND
who serve on the frontline of the Police Service.

and

for my children that they may better understand.

CHAPTER ONE

On the Beat – The "Real" World

I remember the day I first went to inquire about joining the Police Force as clearly as if it was yesterday.

It was a Saturday morning in April 1952. I went to what was then Police Headquarters in James Street Perth. The Training School was a single class-room on the ground floor at the back of the main building. There was a small verandah section leading to a corridor that separated the class-room from the crib-room and locker-room.

I was hesitating on the verandah, a little unsure of my directions when another aspiring applicant joined me. He knew where to go and we walked down the corridor together. This bloke was probably in his mid-twenties, about 6 feet tall and quite well built, whereas I was only 5'9", weighed exactly 10 stone 6 lb and had only recently turned nineteen years of age. I was well aware that I only just met the minimum specifications for acceptance as a probationary constable in the Police Force.

The Officer in Charge of the Police School, First Class Sergeant George Flanders (equivalent rank now Senior Sergeant) answered our knock. He first directed himself to answering the questions of my well-built companion, explaining the entrance examination procedure and medical test applicants were required to undergo. He then turned to me and said, "And what can I do for you, young fellow?"

He seemed surprised when I said that I too wanted to join the Police Force. He challenged both my age and height and even took me into his office to carefully check my weight and height – confirming (as I knew he would) that I did indeed meet the minimum requirements. So the wheels were set in motion, and within a few days I sat for a fairly basic written entrance examination. Then, after obtaining the required number of testimonials and a copy of my birth certificate, I had to wait for the next "call up".

I was optimistic of my acceptance for I had only recently completed my full time National Service training. I knew I was physically fit – so the Medical examination required of applicants posed no problem – and I had been attending night school classes as part of my apprenticeship training, so the written tests were a breeze.

On the strength of my expected entry to the Police Force, I quit the balance of my apprenticeship as a Metal Spinner (one of the poorly paid dying craft trades) and obtained a job as a First Class Wood machinist. Then wonder of wonders, almost at the same time came the offer of fully furnished housing. An elderly family friend was looking for a young married couple to move in with him on a nominal rental, plus housekeeping duties. At a time when young people married and lived for ages with either one's parents until they could find or afford accommodation on their own, it seemed like a dream. So I married "the girl of my dreams" on July 10, 1952 and we moved in.

Appearing before the Selection Board on August 28, 1952, turned out to be quite a trial. Gathered in the courtyard behind Police Headquarters in James street, there were about one hundred men. Each eagerly waiting to go before the Board, and all hoping for selection. Most of them were in their mid- twenties, had strong physiques and appeared to be bursting with confidence. I had felt pretty "cocky" until I saw all these other big strong blokes and, as I was aware only thirty or forty men would be

The teen-age bride and groom. My wife and I leaving the church after our marriage.

This photo was taken several months later, sometime before my transfer to the country.

selected for the next Police Training school, my confidence started to evaporate.

Then as the morning progressed, and so many applicants who had been interviewed rejoined us to joyously announce they had "been accepted subject to passing the medical", my spirits plummeted.

Suddenly it was my turn. First Class Sergeant Flanders ushered me into the room where the Selection Board of the Police Commissioner and two other senior Officers were seated at a table facing me as I entered. The Sergeant instructed me to stand to attention at a line drawn across the centre of the room.

I had only just halted at attention when the Commissioner challenged me. He said, "You're not 5'9"!" ... "Yes I am Sir" I replied. "I don't believe you are!" He continued, "Take your shoes off and get over there, and have the Sergeant check your measurements again." God! It seemed like an inquisition.

I moved over to where Sergeant Flanders was waiting at the side with the height measuring stand. The re-assuring wink and smile he gave me steadied my shaking nerves, as he called "Yes Sir. He is exactly 5'9" in height. I measured him originally myself." Then to me "Resume your position, as before."

"Why do you want to join the Police Force?" asked one of the other Board members... "It has always been my ambition to join the Police Force" I lied, for I hadn't really thought about it until a few months before, but had been told this was the answer they expected. "And I believe the Police Force will provide me with the security and job satisfaction I want."

"Well" said the Commissioner, "You're a bit young and a bit small for what we want. You may have to wait a year or two to get in. What do you think about that? – There's a lot of other blokes out there to choose from and we only want thirty"

"If I have to wait, then I will." I answered, my spirits sinking again.

"Okay. You'll be accepted subject to passing the Medical. But as I said you may have to wait a bit."

With a rather heavy heart I left the room, but Sergeant Flanders who accompanied me to the verandah to call the next applicant encouraged me when he said, "Don't be too worried just yet. They have to pass their Medical and many won't get through. Believe me I know."

There was only a short wait in the courtyard before I was examined by the District Medical Officer and certified fit. But as the Sergeant had predicted, the rejection rate (on medical grounds) was high. In the finish only twenty-eight applicants were accepted, and I was one of them.

*   *   *   *   *

After four months intense training in law, Police procedures, first aid, motor cycle riding and basic unarmed combat, we were on the beat working from Central Police Station in the City area as "probationary constables". At first we worked in pairs with a more experienced beat constable. As the beat constables are the "working pool" from which all staff are drawn or return to (for whatever reason) you worked alongside a range of different characters. Some of the beat constables were in the pool as punishment for some internal misdemeanour, perhaps even reduced in rank as well, others were keen blokes trying to make their mark – to be "noticed" – to enhance further opportunity, and some had only graduated from the school before us.

A Police Force (or "Service" as it is now known) like any other large organisation, is a microcosm of the community from whom its members are drawn. There are workers and drones, good blokes and misfits who are incapable or unsuitable for the job at hand.

As a young beat constable learning his trade, it was often necessary for me to ignore the negative attitude of some of those with whom I worked, and to concentrate on developing a level of confidence in my own ability to be an effective and responsible policeman. The power and authority a policeman assumes on taking office is really quite awesome, and must be exercised responsibly for the police are dealing, not only with the law but also with peoples lives. Although the "without fear or favour" doctrine obviously applies, common- sense and discretion are also a very important part of effective law enforcement.

I remember a fairly typical example that demonstrates this point. Soon after Christmas 1952, not long after we came out of Training School, the Liquor Licensing laws were changed to make "street drinking" (ie. the drinking of liquor in the street, public parks and other places of public resort) illegal. It was a big change and Police policy was to bring in the new law with a "softly softly approach". As beat constables we were instructed to give street drinkers the option of emptying the remainder of their drink on the ground and receiving a caution, or having their particulars taken with a view to prosecution. Of course if they became too "stroppy", they were to be arrested and charged with the offence.

On the afternoon shift (3pm to 11pm), some of the beat constables were rostered to work 4pm to mid-night in plain clothes, with the specific duty of assisting in the implementation of the new law. Unfortunately I was rostered to team up with an objectionable aggressive fellow officer named "Fred." Our individual attitudes were poles apart. Whereas I opted for the "Softly Softly" approach (as I believed we were required to do) Fred wanted to "Lock 'em all up". On several occasions we nearly got into a blue with groups of people we found drinking, simply because of Fred's aggressive manner, but when I intervened and quietly explained the option they co-operated.

As the evening wore on, the atmosphere between Fred and me was less than friendly, because we hadn't made any arrests. Then Fred, who was senior to me and therefore in charge, decided we would check out a wooded area off St George's Terrace which was then part of the grounds of Government House. It was a rough bush area, where men attending functions at Anzac House (almost directly opposite), regularly "planted" a few bottles to quench their thirst between dances. Our Fred was certain we would catch one or two of these blokes illegally drinking in the grounds of Government House. Over the low wall and into the bush we went. It was as dark as the inside of a dog's belly away from the street lights, and when I started to trip over fallen trees, etc, (much to Fred's disgust) I turned on my torch.

"Put that damn thing out!" hissed Fred in a stage whisper, "They'll see us coming"

"Go to buggery! " I replied, "I'm not breakin' a leg just to catch a bloody street drinker."

Obviously the "villains" must have been observing us or heard the exchange between Fred and me, for suddenly there was a noise like a herd of elephants taking off through the bush.

"Stop! Police!" shouted Fred, as he charged off after them with torch in hand: I had no enthusiasm to join him so I simply retraced my steps to the footpath in St George's Terrace. There were blokes flying past me down the footpath like they were trying to escape from all the devils in hell, and in the excitement of the moment I briefly joined in the chase. Then quickly realising this was pointless, I was just slowing to a stop when WHAM! I was flattened by another runner. There was no time for me to get out of his way, nor he to avoid me, as Fred was hot on his heels like a greyhound after a rabbit and I barely had time to partially turn and brace myself before the runner cannoned into me.

As we sprawled together on the footpath winded by the impact, Fred was all over the bloke. Seizing him by the front of his shirt, he snarled. "Got Ya! Thought you'd get away didn't ya'?" Then suddenly recognition dawned on both me and the bloke lying beside me: it was Norm, a big bloke I did my National Service training with before joining the Police Force.

We ignored Fred, who was now almost frothing at the mouth at what he saw as my (again) intervention, and exchanged greetings. "Fancy running into you like this ", said Norm. It gave us both a good laugh, lying there on the footpath. But Fred wasn't laughing and he hadn't finished yet by a long way.

"You were drinking liquor in there weren't you?" He questioned. "Come on you're coming back in there with us to show us what you did with it".

"In where?" asked Norm innocently.

"You F...'n know where! In the bush back there!"

"No I wasn't."

"Well why were you running?"

"I was running to catch me bus"

It was time to intervene. I said "Okay Norm. You better get on your way then, or you'll miss your bus."

Norm got to his feet. Helped me up. We shook hands and he was gone, leaving me to deal with a very irate Fred.

"What the Hell did you let him go for? Just 'cos he's a bloody mate I suppose!"

"And just what do you think we could have charged him with?"

"We could have charged him with loitering"

"Loitering? Loitering? You'd have to be kidding. He certainly wasn't loitering mate! I'd swear to that."

So unhappily we finished our shift, Fred complaining about me to the Sergeant in charge of the Relief, claiming that I "was always letting off my mates and others." However the Sergeant accepted my version of the event(s) and took the matter no further.

In case you're wondering, Fred didn't last long in the Police Force, "resigning" a few years later.

*   *   *   *   *

The Police beat "system", comprises of selected parts of the city divided into grids and allocated a number and time coverage according to particular policing needs and the time of the day. For example one typical beat on night shift encompassed the area bounded by Barrack street, Wellington street, Pier street and Murray street Perth. The time allocated for a Constable to walk this beat was one hour, and you were expected to check all lane-ways and buildings in this locality on each circuit. The Beat (or Relief) Sergeant(s) would meet you from time to time somewhere on your beat to check that everything was okay. The whole city area was divided thus. Most of the beat areas we walked in the 1950's are the same today, although the Northbridge area of the city is now the main focus.

Because of changed community attitudes and policing needs, today's police constables patrol the beat in pairs, particularly on evening and night shift. But in the 1950's the only time you doubled up was when a new school came out. At other times, as staff numbers fluctuated the number of beats manned likewise increased or decreased. As a "rookie", depending on who you worked with, you learnt the short cuts or the importance of checking all the out of the way places on each beat, and who to "look out for" in case you encountered them on your beat.

I remember thinking to myself as I was initially shown up some of these dark alleys and lanes by a more experienced beat constable, that I wouldn't be venturing too far off the street when I worked on my own if could help it. But things change and you soon develop a confidence in yourself and a responsible attitude that compels you to do the job properly – also I suppose there is a degree of boredom involved when you are walking your beat alone, almost in slow motion and nothing is happening (particularly at night). So in a very short time I found myself checking out all these somewhat "spooky" places as a matter of routine. Then at about 3 o'clock one morning I had an experience that frightened the hell out of me.

Between Wellington street and Murray street, there is a small cobblestone lane about 100 metres west of Pier street. About 80 metres up this lane there was a small alley running eastward to service the rear of business premises fronting onto Wellington street. I was up this small alley, at its furthermost point. It was very dark and as I checked out the back of the business premises and yards with my torch, I pushed at the closed door of a toilet with my foot. As the door moved inwards it struck a man lying asleep on the floor. He shouted in alarm, clambered up and still half asleep stumbled towards me as I backed away.

He was a fairly tall aboriginal bloke, with a deep knife scar leading from his forehead to half way down his cheek. The injury had cost him one eye, and the other was wide with terror. I recognised him immediately by this shocking facial scar and his general description. It was Rex Calyan, a bloke other beat constables had warned me about as always wanting to fight police whenever he had been drinking. It was said he "always had a go".

Poor Rex, who couldn't see me behind the torch beam, was obviously as frightened as I was. But I quickly steadied myself and took control... "Police here. What are you doing?" I asked firmly.

"Err... I went for a pee and must have fallen asleep. I'm sorry Constable" an obviously relieved Rex replied. I could smell stale liquor on him but he certainly wasn't drunk.

"Well come on, move out. You can't sleep there" I followed up.

"Yeah yeah, okay"

Then as we were moving back down the lane towards the street lights (me keeping a rather wary eye on Rex, walking alongside) he added "Geez Constable you frightened the hell out of me back there, I nearly died"

With my stampeded heart only just returning to normal, I thought "the feeling's mutual Rex, the feeling's mutual."

*   *   *   *   *

Like any large city, Perth was alive at night with a

range of homeless people derelicts and night-workers, and I'm sure it is basically little different now than it was in the 1950's except that the numbers have increased and the average age of the human flotsam and jetsam may be lower. When you are walking the beat you come to know many of these people well. Some are quite eccentric, some a little mad, and many are in a physical and/or emotional mess through personal circumstances, trauma or alcohol/drug abuse.

It is quite a new experience when you first become a policeman. It certainly was for me. Although I was mature for my age and had a rather Spartan upbringing, nothing – not even the rigour of the Police training school – could have fully prepared me for exposure to the seamy side of life that a policeman often deals with on a daily basis. Until my level of self discipline rose, I had much difficulty in dealing with many of the situations I found myself in, such as handling and searching un-washed vagrants (some alive some dead) as they were admitted to the lock-up or to the mortuary; having to accept that other people's standards of social and moral behaviour often differ greatly from your own; dealing with death and human trauma; trying to cope with severely disturbed persons, and wrestling to control emotions that continually revolted or urged me to react in an undisciplined manner.

Adjusting to shift work for the first time was also quite a problem. Often I came home dog-tired but couldn't sleep because my brain was still trying to come to terms with matters I'd been exposed to during my shift. This was particularly so when working at night. Your "body time clock" kept telling your brain it was time to sleep when you had to be awake.

I remember having a problem like this one night when I was rostered for duty on the Police van. In those days during afternoon (3 -11pm) and night (11pm – 7am) shift there were two Police security vans patrolling the city and inner metropolitan area. Each van had a three man crew, a driver (a constable attached to Transport Section) and a

Sergeant and a Constable from the relief. The Sergeant rode in the front with the driver and the constable rode in the back for the entire shift.

The "Van" wasn't really a van at all, it was a heavy utility with a canvas covered wire cage on the back – much the same as country Police stations have now. The van patrols responded to telephone complaints, or simply patrolled likely trouble areas. It was drafty and uncomfortable riding in the back of the van for an eight hour shift. You had no communication with the Sergeant and driver in the front, the exhaust fumes frequently gave you a head-ache and, in winter, it was very difficult to keep warm. Then one of the "old hands" gave me a tip on how to gain a little comfort. Hanging in the Relief cloak room, there were several old discarded but reasonably clean Police great-coats. Sometimes on a cold night some of the beat constables made use of these if they hadn't brought their own. Apparently if the van crew Sergeant didn't object, the constable riding in the back of the van could use a couple of these old great-coats as blankets to keep himself warm.

I soon organised this "luxury" for myself. With a couple of extra coats wrapped around my legs and lower body I was quite cosy as I settled down for the remainder of my shift. But I was very tired and, as it was a quiet night work-wise, I was soon nodding off to sleep, occasionally slipping sideways on my seat as I battled to remain awake. Finally when I could resist no longer, I laid on the floor covered myself with my "blankets" and was soon fast asleep. In fact I was so deeply asleep I didn't even wake when the van stopped and my mirthful colleagues quietly loaded a drunken vagrant in the back of the van with me. Only when my smelly bed-fellow placed his arm around me attempting to draw me close – saying "C'mon move over and gi'sha bit-a-ya blanket will ya mate" – and the rancid smell of his stale alcohol laden breath and un-washed body cleared the cobwebs from my mind, did I quickly awake. I broke free and roughly pushed him away as I shot to my feet pulling my "blankets" clear. He was obviously concerned at his rejection and surprised I was a policeman, as he said "You don't hav'ta get nasty mate! I only wanted a bit-a-ya blanket. I did'n know ya wash'a bloody coppa!"

He was right of course. You would hardly expect to find a policeman sleeping soundly under a bundle of old clothes on the floor in the back of a Police van, but my reaction was really more embarrassment than anger. The story of my experience exaggerated to add colour and retold by my heart-less work-mates provided humour for several days as it went the rounds at Central.

*　　*　　*　　*　　*

Many old vagrants picked up and charged by police were well and truly on their "last legs"; so physically run down they were only one step away from death. Often their arrest was their one chance to survive – to get them off the street out of the cold and rain with food and shelter at least overnight. When these "old lags" appeared before Court the next day the Magistrate would often sentence them to a short term in gaol, so they would at least get a feed and have somewhere to sleep for a few days. Or they would ask the Magistrate themself for "a few days inside", as they didn't want to "waste" their money on a fine. It always amazed me just how much abuse a human body can take and still survive. Occasionally we found a group of low level vagrants drinking methylated spirit combined with shoe polish, a poisonous concoction which you would expect could kill or at least make them very ill.

I remember one quiet Sunday afternoon as I was on the beat in Wellington Street Perth when I was approached by a tall very frail man in his mid-thirties. He told me he was an alcoholic and pleaded with me to arrest him and lock him up so he would be forced to "dry out" and take treatment. His dark rimmed sunken eyes looked almost life-less, his skin was an ashen colour and there was a strange odour about him – almost like impending death. He told me he had not eaten properly for days and had been drinking watered down methylated spirit (to make the bottle go further). He spoke slowly and rationally and appeared to be a well educated man, but when I suggested that Hospital would be a better option he declined explaining he had tried this but his will-power evaporated as soon as his health improved and he returned to his self destructive former ways.

What a dilemma. The poor bloke had obviously thought it through and considered this was the best way for him. Although he wasn't drunk in the true sense he certainly was affected by liquor and urgently needed help if he was to survive. So I did as he asked and technically arrested him for being "drunk". And as I assisted him to Central Police station and the lock-up it was like walking with a ghost, as though a puff of wind could blow him away like a leaf. I explained the situation fully to the Sergeant in charge and submitted a written report for the information of the Magistrate the following morning. My sad alcoholic got his wish. He was dealt with under the (then) provisions of the Inebriates Act and sentenced to compulsory treatment. I hope he was eventually able to overcome his problem.

Other characters I remember well from my days on the beat – "Percy Buttons", who was once a Circus performer and, in his old age, still did acrobatic feats to entertain people on the streets of Perth for a few pennies. Then there was old "Matches" who sold matches a box at a time usually in Barrack street Perth. He sometimes seemed to lurk in a darkened doorway, stepping out to thrust a box of matches under the nose of an unsuspecting passer-by with a curt query "Matches?" ... "Matches?". And of course who could forget "Little Lennie" a pleasant little Downes Syndrome man who spent each day at the Perth Railway station. Lennie loved trains and knew the regular departure and arrival times of most suburban trains better than anyone. He knew all the Railway staff and most of the regular passengers, whom he would greet with a smile and friendly "G'day" as they passed to or from work. Lennie was like part of the furniture and loved to be asked arrival and departure times so he could proudly demonstrate his knowledge.

*   *   *   *   *

Although night shift on the beat can at times be quite boring, often something quite unexpected happens, and your reaction must be immediate. A funny thing like this happened one morning about 6.30am when I was standing at the corner of Barrack street and Murray street, watching the sleeping city slowly coming to life. I only had about a half hour to go before knocking off at 7am. It had been a long cold night and I was quite weary and looking forward to getting home to bed. Suddenly I heard the clip clop of a horse's hooves and coming down Murray street against the east-bound early morning traffic, I saw a trotter pulling a driver-less trap. It was passing me almost as I saw it.

I snapped out of my lethargic state and took off after it. Although I was rugged up in winter gear, with great-coat scarf and gloves, my sudden sprint enabled me to catch hold of the back of the trap cart. I had no chance of taking hold of the reins (which were dragging on the ground), so I called loudly, "Whoa! whoa!" and tried to steady the horse by pulling on the cart. But instead of slowing, the damn thing took off – it probably thought that I said "Go! Go!".

Although I knew I was bound to fall when I let go, I tried desperately to hang on, until it seemed my feet were no longer touching the ground. Then releasing my grip on the back of the trap cart I went sprawling base over apex on the roadway, much to the amusement of the few early morning workers who had witnessed the chase. Fortunately my heavy clothing saved me from losing too much skin, but I was bruised and dishevelled, and my ego wasn't too flash either.

There were no such niceties as hand-held radios back then, so by the time I reported the matter at Central Police station, no sign of the trotter could be found. Then a day or so later I read a report in the newspaper that the poor creature, which had apparently escaped from its driver during an early morning training trial in East Perth, became involved in a traffic accident in Leederville and had to be destroyed.

*   *   *   *   *

Speaking of encounters with animals there is another unusual incident I remember, that happened one night when I was acting as the Police Guard on night shift at Government House. Although a particular constable held a permanent position as Police Guard at Government House on day shift, Central Police allocated a constable for the afternoon and night relief. The duty constable had a small office near the entrance to the residential section of Government House, and vetted unannounced visitors, took phone calls and monitored the security of the buildings and grounds.

Particularly during the afternoon and night shift the constable on duty was expected to patrol the grounds regularly, checking the security of outbuildings, gates and such like. Each patrol was recorded in the office "Occurrence Book" and checked by the Relief Sergeant. Late night road traffic noise and other activity was minimal in those days, and on a still night you could often hear the lions roaring across the Swan River at the South Perth Zoo.

This particular night at about 4am, I was making one of my routine patrols of the grounds and had just checked the last gate on the far end of the back fence (the South East corner of the grounds). In this area there were several plant nursery hot-houses and machinery sheds. I checked the padlock on the gate, turned my back and walked five or six paces when suddenly the roar of a lion shattered the silence of the night. The intensity of the sound, suggested it was only feet away from me. I nearly died of fright. They say that when you are about to meet your maker, your life flashes before you. It's true ... I could see the newspaper headlines "CONSTABLE DIES FIGHTING ESCAPED LION WITH BATON".

With the hair on the back of my neck sticking up like the spines on an echidna, and legs shaking like jelly I flashed my torch about in the inky darkness trying to see where the attack might come from as I quickly made my way back to the office. "Don't run. Don't panic!" I kept telling myself. Then phew, I made it and closed the door. Later as I calmed down and thought rationally again I asked myself "How could it be? Perhaps I imagined it? It simply didn't seem possible. If a lion did escape from the Zoo it could hardly swim the river (there was no Narrows Bridge then) and be lurking in the grounds of Government House. There had to be a logical explanation. And of course there was. As daylight dawned and I returned to the lower garden area where I had been earlier, I saw that a circus group was camped on the esplanade behind Government House. The lion cages being stationed only a foot or two from the back fence very close to the last gate I checked. Apparently "King Leo" didn't take kindly to me disturbing his sleep, and voiced his disapproval.

*   *   *   *   *

Occasionally beat constables were rostered for various other duties like assisting on Point duty or as a Court orderly, Prisoner escort or Guard duty. The latter included times when a 24 hour hospital guard was placed on un-sentenced prisoners receiving treatment in a public hospital. Guarding a prisoner in hospital was particularly stressful. It was not a duty we enjoyed. You had to maintain a very high level of alertness throughout the entire eight hour shift. You were on your own and the prisoner you were guarding was usually a violent and/or dangerous person. On at least two occasions I guarded prisoners who had committed murder then failed in an attempt to take their own life. They often wanted to tell you their story: the pathetic circumstances that led them to their crime. It was sometimes hard not to feel sympathy, but you could not afford to relax your vigilance.

I remember one particular bloke who was very difficult to guard. A confidence trickster who had some medical knowledge, he had been posing as a qualified Doctor in several states of Australia. When arrested in Perth on a series of fraud charges, and in custody awaiting trial, he attempted suicide and was transferred to Royal Perth Hospital under Guard. He was a very persuasive cunning man, and made several further "apparent" attempts on his life while under Police guard in Hospital – using a range of sharp instruments acquired from lord knows where to open major arteries on his body before being detected. I have used the word "apparent", when referring to this bloke's attempts to take his life, as we were never sure whether he was dinkum or not. But he sure got a lot of us into trouble for not taking sufficient care to prevent him from injuring himself.

Point duty; directing and controlling the flow of traffic through the major city intersections, was one of the more "sought after" tasks for the beat constables. It was then years before Traffic Control lights were installed, and even today I believe a good "Pointsman" can do a better job than the lights when traffic is heavy. The "Pointsmen Squad", a group of constables permanently appointed for such duty, manned the intersections during the day, but at other times (or when a Pointsman was absent on leave) the beat constables took over the task.

Electric trams and trolley buses still operated in the city in those days and the Pointsman had to step to the edge of the small square mat on which he stood to allow clearance for a tram to pass. One of the "traps for young players" was to forget you had nowhere to go if you waved two opposing trams on at once. Many of us "new chums"

19

got caught in this embarrassing situation, but fortunately the tram drivers usually knew the score and wouldn't move until it was safe for them to do so.

It was a great feeling to stand in the centre of a major city intersection directing traffic. Some of the Pointsmen really looked quite majestic, as with precise arm movements and military precision they timed their signals to keep traffic flowing with minimum delay. People would often stand for ages and watch a Pointsman's skilful rhythmic display.

*   *   *   *   *

Then if you were lucky (as I was) you could be picked to act as the permanent "runner" with one of the C.I.B. night motor patrols. This was a very sought after exciting position. It gave you the chance to gain valuable experience and work with the detectives. To become "known". It could also enhance your chances of later selection (if such was your chosen career path) for the Criminal Investigation Branch. Two beat constables were chosen from each relief, and each time the relief was on night shift you worked in plain clothes with a detective. There were only two night motor patrols, each with a detective or detective sergeant, a driver from the Police transport pool, and the constable selected as runner. One patrol worked from 6pm to 2am, and the other from 10pm to 6am.

The C.I.B. night motor patrols were the first to respond to any report of major crime occurring in the city and metropolitan area. The runner's job was to operate the radio and record incoming messages. You went with the detective as he attended the crime scene and interviewed the persons involved. The title "runner" also meant what it said – if an offender tried to run away to escape apprehension, it was the runner's job to catch him. As you were the younger and usually more agile member of the team, on arrival at a scene, the runner was often the first over the fence into the back yard or where-ever.

It was often exciting stuff, and the adrenalin would be pumping through your veins at peak pressure. Because of the dangerous nature of the work each member of the team was armed with a .38 calibre revolver carried in a shoulder holster, loaded and ready for use. In recent years it has become compulsory for members of the Police Service at all levels to have regular weapons training, but it has not always been so. Although I did receive training in the use of military type weapons during my National Service and had basic shooting practice using a revolver in the Police school, I was not really all that familiar with the mechanism of a revolver – a factor which very nearly resulted in tragedy.

One night shortly after mid-night, when our patrol was cruising in the suburb of Maylands, I received an "offender on premises" message on the Police radio. The premises were those of a small Delicatessen on Great Eastern Highway, at the corner of Belgravia street Belmont. Our driver, Constable Ken George, had us there within minutes. Parking in the side street we silently approached the building. The front entrance door was secure, but through the darkened shop-front window we could see the beam of a small torch moving about inside. As entrance had obviously been gained from the rear, Detective Sergeant Gordon Moorman posted me to remain by the front door to prevent the offender's escape by that exit, and Ken George was directed to watch the fence-line abutting Belgravia street, while Gordon went over the front fence to check the back of the building. Within a minute or so the torch beam inside the shop went out, followed almost immediately by incoherent shouting and thumping noises as Gordon obviously tackled whoever was inside. Suddenly Ken George was alongside me. He had his revolver in his hand.

"Quick!" he said "Over the fence and round the back. They're half killing Gordon in the back room!" (THEY? that meant there must be more than one) I was over the fence in a flash, and running across the yard towards the back of the shop. In the semi-darkness I saw the figure of a man running towards the back fence. I dived on him quickly subduing him with a head lock/choke hold, just as another figure sped past and tried to scale the rear fence. I scrambled to my feet, with the first bloke struggling to break free from the pressure applied by my left arm held firmly around his throat, and drew my revolver threatening to shoot the second man now trying to scale the fence and escape. There was a lot of shouting going on behind me, and I heard a firearm discharge. The bloke on the fence dropped back to the ground. Then, as he saw I was still struggling with his mate, he apparently decided to make a run for it and started to move sideways. I heard Det/Sergt Moorman call out from somewhere in the darkness "Give the bastard a bullet if he runs!"

I never thought for a minute that he really meant me to shoot the man. It was part of the bluff I had been enacting. But I realised that I may have to fire a warning shot to stop the offender from running. And this is where it all nearly came unstuck. You see in accordance with general practise, I had only loaded my revolver with five bullets leaving the trigger hammer on an empty chamber, in case the weapon was dropped accidentally. In the stress of the moment I thought that the first time I pulled the trigger, the hammer would fall on the empty chamber before moving to the next live round, completely forgetting that the chamber revolves and fires the next shot in one action as you pull the trigger. It all happened in the skip of a heart-beat. There I was, holding one struggling man with my left arm, my wobbly revolver pointing directly at the middle of the second offender less than ten feet away, when I pulled the trigger and the weapon discharged with a boom and flash of flame in the darkness.

The bloke under my arm suddenly went limp (the gun was close to his head when it went off) and the man in front of me dropped to the ground. I really thought I'd shot him as, releasing the choke-hold on the bloke under my arm and re-holstering my revolver, I rushed forward to examine the inert form lying on the ground. But somehow I'd missed him (probably because of my unsteady stance).

Although he was frightened half to death at nearly being shot, the poor bloke quickly recovered and Det/Sergt Moorman, who joined me within seconds of the shot being fired, arrested both men and handcuffed them together. A third offender had been caught by Constable George outside the fence. The first shot I heard had been fired by the Constable as the man attempted to attack him with a tyre lever he had already successfully used on the sergeant.

The sequence of the event commenced when Gordon Moorman first got to the back of the building. He found the rear door jemmied open and entered the back room, turning on the light as he did so. To use his words – "I switched on the light and a bloke ran out of the next room so I grabbed him. Next minute another one appeared and they both started to bash me. One had a tyre lever. I was holding onto them and yelling like hell for you blokes to join me when another one appeared out of the darkness and I thought, Geez they're coming at me on an escalator belt. I was still yelling out and copping plenty when they broke free. I was fairly dazed as I followed the last one out through a hole in the fence. That's when Ron grabbed him. I looked back into the yard and saw you with the other two, one about to make a run for it. I yelled to give him a shot and suddenly there was a bang and he dropped like a stone. I really thought you'd shot him. It was so close. Too close."

Fortunately Det/Sergt Moorman was not seriously injured, and after the matter (my accidental discharge of the revolver) was fully investigated, I was not charged with any offence. It could so easily have gone the other way. The man could have been dead or injured and my life too ruined. Even after so many years I still get goose-bumps when I think of it. I remained on the beat for a little over twelve months, and during that period I spent a short time on relief duty at the Belmont Police station, and also the old Guildford Police station (now a museum) then, as it was my ambition to become a "Country Cop" in January 1954 I successfully applied for the position of second man at the Goomalling Police station, in the Eastern Wheatbelt Region of Western Australia. When I took up my posting early in February, I had just turned twenty one years of age and been in the Police Force for seventeen months, having only recently completed my twelve months probationary period. I still looked very young and, although I had a wife and baby son by then, many of the locals thought at first that I was the new policeman's son.

CHAPTER TWO

Country Posting – A Start in the Bush

I was on night shift when one of the relief Sergeants told me he'd heard there was a vacancy for the second constable position at Goomalling. He said he'd "put a word in for me" with the Staff Office Sergeant but I would need to confirm that I wanted the posting as soon as possible in the morning. So I telephoned Staff Office soon after it opened at 8am and spoke with the Sergeant in charge. Then later in the day (as instructed) I presented myself for interview. This turned out to be a little unusual, as I was taken "up the golden stairs" and spoken to by Commissioner Anderson himself. He asked me a few routine questions about how I liked the Police Force, etc., and where my ambitions lay. Then he asked the one question I had been dreading, "What motor vehicle do you have?"

Now in the 1950's nearly all of the few vehicles owned and operated by the Police Department were stationed in the Perth metropolitan area. The exception being the motor cycles and side-cars provided for Detectives stationed at the larger country centres. Elsewhere in the state the private vehicles of policemen were used. At each station and centre a certain officer was designated as the "Inquiry Man" or "Day Reserve" and his vehicle was used for policing purposes on a contract mileage basis. Of course official use of the vehicle was monitored and strictly controlled.

At Goomalling the second man position was the Inquiry Man and the contract amount was eight pounds ten shillings per month for a maximum of 130 miles. Any mileage over this figure was paid for on a sliding scale as "excess mileage". Financially there was little gain for the constable concerned as he was responsible for all maintenance and repairs, including any damage incurred on official business. About the only benefit was that the nominated officer was able to apply for a State Treasury loan to purchase a vehicle duty free through Government Stores. So when Commissioner Anderson asked me what vehicle I had, it was with some trepidation I nervously replied, "A 1931 model Austin Seven, Sir"

"Good lord. An Austin Seven. Do you really think that would be suitable for police inquiry work?"

"Yes Sir" I replied, with more confidence than I felt, trying not to think of the un-sealed corrugated roads, "It's well shod and in very good mechanical condition. I'm sure it will do the job."

"Are you in a position to buy something more suitable?" He questioned.

"Not at present, Sir", I held my breath as he pondered my reply.

"Well okay then, but just as soon as you are, put in a report and I'll approve it. Alright then you can have the position at Goomalling. The Staff Office Sergeant will arrange the details"

And so I was away, elated at being accepted for my first country posting and the opportunity to gain a wealth of experience I believed would enhance my prospects of further advancement.

Looking back I have mixed feelings about Goomalling. As a young policeman I found most of the townspeople a fairly "cliquey" group. Our Government owned house was on a large block in an isolated position on the edge of town. We had no phone (couldn't afford one) and no close

The Austin 7, with wife June standing alongside.

neighbours. With only basic material possessions and little money over after rather heavy superannuation payments and hire purchase commitments had been met, it was a long hard grind to improve our situation. We had very little social life.

Perhaps had we belonged to the predominant church group or been able to join a sporting club together things may have been different. But with a very young family the nature of my employment, intermittent duties and frequent absences on relief duty elsewhere this was not possible. It was an isolated and lonely life, particularly for my wife when I was away relieving at other stations for periods ranging from a few days to six weeks at a time. Many police marriages perish under conditions such as this – that ours didn't is a tribute to the quality of our relationship.

*   *   *   *   *

At about the time of my transfer to Goomalling there had been a complete change of staff. The Constable in charge died and the second man had been transferred to an Officer in charge position at another station. So when I got there I worked for a couple of months under a senior constable who was temporarily filling the O.I.C. position until the arrival of my new boss Constable Cedric Vernon Eaton (known to everyone as "Tubby"). As the name suggests, Tubby was a huge rotund man 6'2" (187.96cm) weighed 21 stone (133.35kg), and even though he carried more weight than he should have he was not flabby. With our contrasting size we looked a rather odd pair.

With Tubby's arrival it became obvious that my little Austin 7 was not suitable for police work. In fact when Tubby first saw the little car he snorted and said, "What! How in hell do you think I'm going to fit in that?" Of course it was out of the question so, as I wanted to retain the car hire contract, I had to move quickly and purchase a more suitable vehicle. Although our limited finances were already stretched I obtained a Treasury loan and bought a second-hand Austin A 70 utility.

Aged about thirty five at that time, Tubby was born and raised in Goomalling, where he excelled as a member of the local football team. He joined the Police force from Goomalling and his mother and other family members still lived in the town, so he was welcomed as a returning favourite son – particularly when he agreed to coach the local football team. Tubby was a likeable man and a very fair policeman who knew his job well. Paradoxically he was also quite lazy and prided himself in never doing anything he could organize someone else to do.

There were many times during our four year association when my work-load seemed excessive and his attitude unfair; times when I needed to remind myself that, regardless of our disproportionate work loads, I was being paid to work and so I should. It was not until some years later, when I was in charge of my own station, that I fully appreciated how fortunate I had been so early in my career to work under the supervision of someone of Tubby's capability. He was a self-assured decisive man who always seemed to know exactly what had to be done in any situation. And although he never let me forget who was "the boss" he was no bully, and always used persuasion to ensure that whatever I did was done properly. I learnt well under Tubby's guidance and soon became a confident young officer with a good grasp of police station management.

*　　*　　*　　*　　*

Tubby's wife Doreen was a wiry "no nonsense" ex-army girl who could have mixed it with the best of them. She thought the world of Tubby. Born in the goldfields Doreen had a heart of gold and a spirit to match, never afraid to call a basic gardening implement "a bloody shovel" or to use any other expletive she thought suitable for the occasion. As we weren't on the phone, if Tubby (and later his replacement Constable Bob Gilchrist) wanted me at night in an emergency, he would drive to my home to get me sounding the car horn as he turned the corner about 100 yards away. Sometimes it was Doreen who came to call me out if Tubby was on sick leave with the flu or what-ever.

I have always been a light sleeper so as soon as I heard the car horn I would be out of bed in a flash, pull on my police great-coat over my pyjamas, grab my handcuffs, cap and slippers or shoes and meet the car as it pulled up at our gate. Depending on the nature of the task I could be away until morning or return within the hour, you just never knew.

It was funny one night when I turned out thus – dressed in my "turn-out gear". In those days there were "Railway Refreshment Rooms" at various railway stations throughout the state, providing food and drink (including alcoholic beverages) for passengers travelling or about to travel on the railway. Goomalling was one such station and, whenever convenient, we attended the railway station at about the time of the train's arrival and departure to support the Train Conductor or Refreshment Room Manager in case of trouble. Usually it was only a case of "showing the flag".

On this occasion during the Christmas holiday season some of the passengers on a train passing through Goomalling after midnight were "well under the weather" and giving the Conductor a hard time, so the Station-master phoned the Police station for assistance. Tubby was ill in bed with the flu so Doreen, clad only in night-attire – as there was no time for her to dress, came up in the car for me. With slippers on, great-coat over my pyjamas and hand-cuffs in my pocket she whisked me off to the railway station. But as we pulled up I realised that in my haste I'd forgotten my Police cap.

"Here use Tubby's" said Doreen, passing me Tubby's police cap which was in the back of the car.

Now remember as Tubby was quite a large bloke, his cap was about three sizes too big for me – so it is just as well God gave me ears or I wouldn't have been able to see. Undaunted by my appearance I stormed onto the platform among the milling crowd, trying to look serious as I searched for the Conductor up and down the train to see what help he needed.

It was quite a warm night. The passengers (many a little tipsy) were in a festive mood and cheered my arrival amongst them. I knew how crazy I must have looked – feet encased in carpet slipper; pyjama-clad legs protruding from beneath my winter great-coat, and an oversize Police cap adorning my head. I found it difficult not to join in their laughter in fact I nearly cracked-up as one character leant out of a carriage window and, seeing me going past in my odd gear, shouted to his mates "Hey man! Dig the crazy rig on the Square!"

The Conductor's problem was minimal. I sorted it out and the train was soon on its way. As Doreen drove me back home, we had a good laugh about the whole incident. We agreed that, as she was wearing only flimsy summer night-wear, it would have seemed even more outlandish had I made an arrest.

The Goomalling Railway Station/Railway Refreshment Room building. Closed November 1989.

CHAPTER THREE

Piney's Mob

The static Aboriginal population at Goomalling was relatively small, about twenty or thirty adults and at least the same number of children. With one or two exceptions they were generally law abiding citizens and only came under the notice of Police when affected by drink. Aboriginal/Police relations were good.

Some Government Aboriginal Housing was just becoming available in the townsite, but most of the people still lived on the Aboriginal Reserve on the other side of the railway line. There was no proper housing, running water or toilet facilities and families lived there in small tin humpys made of corrugated iron sheeting or flattened oil drums. Yet, in spite of these primitive conditions, (and great credit to the women) the Aboriginal children were generally clean and regularly attended school. Although some of the men were employed full time with the Railway maintenance gang or the local Council, most were employed as seasonal farm labourers. Some of them were particularly good shearers and could make big money at shearing time.

One on-going problem the town and surrounding farms had with the people on the Reserve was their reluctance to control dog numbers. Every family had several dogs and breeding went unchecked. Many dogs were underfed, some starving and scrounging for food in the town, or worse still forming a pack to attack sheep on close-by farms. The havoc they created was quite sickening. Properties adjacent to town were the most affected and the police were regularly called on for help. It would be bad enough if domestic dogs on a rampage killed and ate to satisfy their hunger, but once the frenzy starts they seem to keep on and on maiming and tearing for what seems to be the excitement and sheer pleasure of it.

I remember a period when dog numbers on the Reserve seemed rather high and hardly a week went by without at least one report of dogs attacking sheep. I'd grab the station rifle (a .44 calibre 15 shot Winchester lever action saddle carbine) and head off to meet the farmer concerned, trying to shoot the dog or dogs involved before they left the property, and, although I sometimes managed to shoot one or two, in most instances I missed. It wasn't that I had any real pity for the renegade dog – you only had to see or remind yourself of the horrific injuries they inflicted on the helpless sheep to tighten your resolve. It was more like I couldn't have hit a barn door with a handful of wheat I seemed to be such a crook shot. Sometimes I was so close I could have jumped out of the car and hit the damn dog with a stick – but somehow I still missed. Then came the night (and morning) when the scenario changed.

At about nine one night Tubby and I were at a function of some sort when Gerry Locker (known locally as "the beard" because of his bushy black whiskers) came and asked for our help as a pack of dogs were attacking his sheep in paddocks adjacent to the town and close to where I lived. In view of my dismal record as a marksman I almost pleaded with Tubby to go with Gerry himself. "No. No. You'll do alright. Off you go." he said, ignoring my plea.

Back to the station to get the Winchester 44 and a packet of bullets and I was off with Gerry in his ute to the farm. We quickly located the marauding dogs herding and attacking a mob of about one hundred sheep. In the darkness there seemed to be dogs everywhere, at least a dozen or so barking and tearing at the poor creatures trying to huddle together for protection. I was on the back of Gerry's moving ute and he was using a spotlight as he drove, pinpointing dogs for me to shoot at. It was a shambles. What with swirling dust, dogs and sheep all mixed up and the unsteadiness of my shooting platform I failed again. I might have hit one or two but none of them dropped as they scattered in the darkness. I was thoroughly disgusted with myself.

As I helped Gerry collect his twenty or so badly injured sheep (most of them being either dead or dying) he asked me to retain the gun and ammunition at my home, as he expected the dogs to return later that night or early in the morning. I agreed but suggested he would probably do better working alone with his rifle, for I'd been no help at all. But Gerry had more confidence in me than I had, and said he'd probably be back for me around daybreak.

I was quickly awake at the sound of the car horn. Dawn was just breaking as I ran out in slippers and pyjamas with the rifle and ammunition to join Gerry – this time driving his FJ Holden sedan. His property was just across the road from my home and we were on the scene within a minute or two. Gerry had been right. It was a replay of the previous night's sickening mayhem. The dogs were there in numbers racing about barking, slashing and tearing into the poor helpless sheep huddled together in the paddock. But this time it all came together for me and I couldn't miss. Gerry drove the FJ like a man possessed as we raced around the paddock, sliding and wheeling to cut off lines of escape and setting his car in position for my best chance of a hit on a dog. None escaped. Within minutes we had twelve (very dead) dogs accounted for. And to everyone's relief (other than their owners) the dog population on the Aboriginal Reserve was temporarily reduced.

Gerry "The Beard" Lockyer. Photo taken in 1953.

*   *   *   *   *

The Aboriginal people on the reserve were family oriented and always seemed to get back together again fairly quickly even after a real ding-dong blue. Many of the children were good at sports and some of the teenagers were first class footballers. The main family group was the Walleys. Piney was the "Elder" and he and Eileen had eleven children. Then came the Dicks and the Pontons. Various relations and others floated in and out from time to time to swell the population. There were no "full blood" Aboriginals at Goomalling, most were classed (under the

Native Welfare Act) as "half castes" or "quadroons" and, as this was the era before the Aboriginal people of Australia were granted full citizenship, some had "Citizen's Rights" and some didn't.

Under the provisions of the (then) Native Welfare Act and the Liquor Licensing Act, a person classed as an "Aboriginal" was prohibited from entering licensed premises and purchasing or receiving liquor. It was likewise an offence to sell or supply liquor to an "Aboriginal".

"Citizen's Rights" as it was known, was really like a passport as it contained a photograph and personal details of the holder. A "Certificate of Citizenship" (the correct name) entitled a person to whom it was granted the same rights and obligations as any other member of the community. Sadly, many Aboriginal people considered the most important "right" they gained was the legal right to enter Licensed Premises and drink and or purchase liquor. In fact many actually referred to the Certificate of Citizenship as their "Drinking Rights".

Strictly speaking (by law) an Aboriginal person who had Citizen's Rights was not permitted to live on the Aboriginal Reserve or to cohabit with "Natives" (Native Welfare Act). It was a crazy law which I doubt was ever fully enforced by Police. It certainly wasn't in my time at country police stations. Of course those Aboriginal people who had legal access to alcohol shared it (or refused to share it) with their neighbours. It was a difficult situation either way as alcohol was invariably the major cause of the many squabbles and fights on the Reserve.

I always felt sorry for the women. Most didn't drink alcohol themselves and battled very hard to maintain a stable existence for their family. Sometimes the fighting between people on the Reserve became quite violent and serious injury could result. As soon as trouble seemed likely the ladies never hesitated. They came to the Police station or sent one of their kids for us and we would go over to the Reserve and try to sort it out. At times a warning would suffice and the matter could be settled peacefully, but often we arrested and charged the main culprit as there was no alternative. The situation "Andy" created and his subsequent behaviour, which culminated in a hefty prison sentence, clearly demonstrates this point.

It was mid-afternoon on a Saturday and I had just spent a pleasant hour or so washing and polishing my recently purchased second-hand Austin A.70 utility. The paintwork had really come up well with a cut and polish and I was pleased with my efforts. Then my high spirits faded as one of the Aboriginal kids arrived at the Police station to tell me that "Andy" was drunk and causing trouble on the Reserve. Andy was not a local Aboriginal although he was related to one of the families. He was a young man aged about twenty, and rather keen on one of the teen-age girls living on the Reserve. When much younger he apparently had some success as a boxer with the Police & Citizens Youth Club and when affected by drink was inclined to want to "take on the world". In fact only a few months before, when I was questioning him about some minor offence on the Reserve, he suddenly knocked me flat with a blow to my right temple, splitting my eye-brow. Duly arrested and charged with assaulting me, Andy had been sentenced to a period of imprisonment. He had only just returned to Goomalling a few days earlier on his discharge from prison and here he was again causing trouble. Although we didn't always have a backup when going to a complaint on the Reserve it was a general rule that, whenever possible, Tubby and I attended together. So I went to the football club where Tubby was supervising training exercises and picked him up in my ute. As we drove onto the Reserve and up towards the humpy where we had been told we would find Andy, I could see a dozen or so people standing in a rough circle well clear of the dwelling. Then before my vehicle came to a stop Andy suddenly rushed towards us from the building. He was bare-footed, shirt-less, screaming at the top of his voice and swinging a shovel around his head like a mad Highlander with a Claymore rushing to his death.

As I was braking to a stop Andy swung the shovel in a sideways chopping motion to strike the front of the vehicle – my oh so beautiful Austin A.70 – with such force that it cut through the metal bodywork close to the headlight. It was unbelievable. I was out of the vehicle in a flash (afterwards Tubby said he wasn't sure if I even paused to open the door). Foolishly I suppose, my immediate priority was to see what damage had been done, completely ignoring Andy who was still swinging the shovel about and shouting incoherently.

"What the hell did you do that for?" I bellowed in anger, "Look what you've done to my bloody car!"

I think Andy was quite surprised that I was more worried about the damage he'd done than in tackling him. He lowered the shovel, stopped yelling and joined me to look at the gash he'd made in the front of the vehicle. Tubby, who was more concerned about my safety than the damage to the vehicle, grabbed Andy as soon as he lowered the shovel and moved forward. There wasn't much of a struggle from Andy (who was only a little smaller than me) with Tubby on one side and me on the other. We took him back to the Police station and placed him in the exercise yard of the lock-up, charged with Creating a Disturbance on the Reserve and Wilful Damage to my vehicle. He had nothing in the pockets of the long trousers he wore, and although obviously affected by liquor he wasn't really drunk and seemed to have calmed down.

When we were in the office completing the paperwork connected with Andy's arrest, he called me by name saying he wanted to "talk to me". I came out in answer to his call and, standing by the corrugated iron outer wall of the exercise yard, I told him to go ahead and talk, as I was listening.

"No, I want you to come in here and talk to me," he said.

"No I won't." I replied, "I can talk to you quite well from out here."

"Well I want you to bring me in a drink of water," he continued.

About this time I looked through a strategically positioned nail hole in the exercise yard wall, that we used for observation purposes. I saw Andy standing flat against the inner wall near the door. He had pulled up one of the wooden steps (previously embedded in the unsealed floor of the exercise yard) and had this heavy plank raised above his head waiting for me to open the door. Silently signalling Tubby to join me from the office and to observe Andy's intentions, I called out "Okay. Wait a minute and I'll get you a drink."

As Tubby opened the door I moved quickly through the opening into the exercise yard, avoiding Andy's blow with the plank. Again it wasn't much of a contest as Tubby and I quickly subdued Andy and put him in a cell. As soon as we closed and locked the door he went berserk again, screaming abuse and obscenities at us and bashing the cell bucket against the walls of the cell.

With Andy now properly secured – the cell door and the exercise yard padlocked – it seemed quite safe to resume our normal activities. I was to return home to spend a few hours with my family and on my way dropped Tubby back at football training. I started for home then changed my mind, as I felt uneasy about Andy and wondered if he had settled down since we left him ten minutes or so before. How lucky for Andy that I did for, as I pulled into the yard of the Police station, I saw black smoke pouring from the wooden cell block. The lock-up was on fire; Andy was inside, and Tubby had the keys to the two heavy padlocks securing the outer and inner doors. I spun my vehicle in a tight turn and headed for the football oval about a half mile away as fast as I could, sounding the car horn in static alarm. As I braked to a stop Tubby was in and we were away back to the station. Then while Tubby hurried to unlock the doors, I organized the garden hose.

Andy semi-conscious with smoke inhalation was

dragged from the cell. The cell mattress and blanket which were well alight were extinguished and dragged into the yard. Fortunately the cell floor and wall were only scorched as they hadn't fully caught alight. A much subdued Andy (who quickly recovered) was placed in another cell with fresh bedding and cell bucket.

The matches? Well yes ... another lesson: never take anything for granted. When we initially searched Andy before putting him in the exercise yard we found nothing in the pockets of the trousers he was wearing. But we didn't notice he was also wearing a pair of shorts under the trousers and in the pocket of the shorts he had matches. In his alcohol affected state, Andy thought he'd get back at the Police by burning down the lock-up. It obviously never occurred to him that he would burn with it. And he very nearly did.

Of course when Andy appeared before Court on the several damage charges involved he received a gaol sentence again. I have often wondered whether he realised just how close to death he came. But drama like this was rare, and usually only arose when "a visitor" from out of town – as is so often the case – wanted to show the locals how good he was.

On another occasion I recall, a melee taking place on the Reserve one night involving a group of about eight male adults belting each other with bottles and short lengths of water pipe simply stopped as soon as I arrived (alone). No Police action was necessary. I finished up taking a car-load of them to the Hospital to have their scalp wounds stitched and dressed. You would have thought they had just come from a pleasant party as they laughed and joked with each other and the Doctor as he stitched them up. All of them had been drinking and were in various stages of sobriety. None had a life threatening or particularly serious injury. Nor did any of them want Police action. I think they probably gave as good as they got and were equally to blame. I am sure they were just glad I arrived and stopped the melee when I did.

The old Goomalling Police station and Court House, now a garage/ storeroom at the Police quarters – used until the opening of the present Police station/Court complex in February 1965. The lockup was adjacent at the rear where the back fence (on the right of the photo) now stands.

*   *   *   *   *

One particular trait I admired in the Aboriginal wives was their firm resolve not to accept domestic violence. One of the on-going frustrations I experienced as a policeman was having to deal with women who were regularly "bashed" by their husband and who refused to take firm action under the law to prevent it. Instead the victim often expected police to call time after time to "warn" the man. Not so with the Aboriginal wives at Goomalling. If they received a belting and called for police help, there was rarely any doubt about whether they wanted the husband arrested and charged. It was more or less standard procedure.

Ironically the family was sometimes better off if the husband was charged, particularly if he received a jail

41

sentence. This may sound crazy but it is a fact. You see if the husband was "serving time" the Native Welfare Dept authorized the local "Protector of Natives" (the constable in charge of the Police station) to issue weekly food vouchers for his family. There was a detailed schedule that set out the various food items and allocation per person. We simply filled in the amounts, the name of the recipient, the grocery store (or Butcher), and authorized the issue. The amounts allocated were quite generous. And the store would often substitute some chosen item of a similar value for a less practical item on the schedule – for example there was not a lot that could be done each week with a large quantity of flour, whereas tins of fruit and other goodies could be used or stored for Dad's welcome-home party.

During my time at Goomalling, Piney's large family was probably the major beneficiary of this scheme. Piney, a quietly spoken big man, was probably in his early forties. He was a family man and rarely got involved in the many petty squabbles of others on the reserve. He didn't "tell tales" or call us in to help settle problems. Likewise he didn't provide police with much information either when we were trying to establish who was at fault following a dispute on the Reserve. You could say he was a solitary man.

Piney had Citizen's Rights and was generally a moderate beer drinker. He was never a problem at the hotel and if he did seem to be getting a bit under the weather, a word from the bar-staff (or Police) was all that was needed and he'd be on his way without too much protest. But despite his seemingly docile manner, Piney had a dark side and occasionally acted quite violently towards his wife Eileen. These outbursts seemed to occur on a fairly regular basis, about every six to twelve months.

Because Piney was a repeat offender, he usually ended up with a jail sentence. The Justices mostly assessed the period of his detention by the severity of his assault on Eileen. He often served his time in the Goomalling Police lock-up and was a model prisoner. In his youth Piney played

42

competition football with Tubby and they were still good friends. So the usual "Gaoler/prisoner" relationship didn't quite fit, with Piney being treated in many ways almost like one of the family. He had the same meals Doreen prepared for Tubby and the kids; if we had hot buttered scones for morning tea, so did Piney. If I took Piney with me for an afternoon gathering firewood, on the way back to the lock-up (having dropped the load off at home), it was understood that I would park for a short time in the rear courtyard of the Hotel, while we shared a cold drink in the car.

While Piney was in our lock-up his family always visited in the afternoon and although there was no obvious "hanky-panky" it was claimed Piney once told some of his friends the Goomalling lock-up was the only one he knew of where you could get your wife pregnant.

I remember well one particularly violent attack Piney made on Eileen. They had apparently argued earlier in the evening and were sitting on empty oil drums by their outside fire, Eileen nursing their two month old baby and Piney silently brooding about lord knows what. He got up from where he was sitting and went off in the dark. Eileen believing the argument was over, thought he had gone to get some wood for the fire. He certainly went to get wood but it wasn't for the fire. The branch of the tree he dragged back (it was as thick as a man's upper-arm) was to use as a club on Eileen. Swinging the branch with two hands as in the action of a baseball player, Piney struck Eileen across the back of the head knocking her and the baby into the fire. Fortunately they received only minor burns, but Eileen's deep scalp wound needed stitching. I interviewed her at the Hospital where she and the baby were being attended to by the Doctor. Eileen, whose main concern was the baby, explained what had taken place and requested that Piney be charged with assault. She knew the procedure well as she had taken this same action several times before.

I found Piney sitting by himself by the fire outside

their humpy. He freely admitted striking Eileen with the tree branch, now lying on the ground close-by, but said he hadn't meant to knock her and the baby into the fire. He made no protest when I arrested him on the assault charge in fact he expected to be arrested, and pleaded guilty (as he always did) when he appeared before Court the following morning. Piney's wry comment to the Bench before sentencing clearly demonstrated his casual attitude and lack of remorse. It would have been funny if the matter hadn't been so serious. As is the practice, one of the two Justices of the Peace read out the charge and asked Piney how he wanted to plead.

"Er... Guilty I suppose. But it was only a bita'va hargument with the missus your warship," he replied.

"Yes... well you'll have a chance to speak about that in a minute. Are you pleading guilty or not guilty?" the Justice continued.

"Guilty... I suppose." said Piney. Then as the court procedure requires, I read out a statement of the facts related to me by Eileen, confirmed by the Doctor and my own inquiries. I dragged the blooded tree branch exhibit forward to be viewed by the Justices and Piney.

"Do you agree with what the Constable said?" asked the Justice, "Do you agree that you hit your wife with this branch?"

"Oh yes," Piney replied, "But I only hit her once! It was only a bita'va hargument."

So for his "bita'va hargument" Piney, because of his long record of convictions for almost identical behaviour, was sentenced to six months imprisonment. But before he left Goomalling to serve his time elsewhere Eileen came to see him and brought the baby and the rest of the kids to say goodbye. There was no animosity what-so-ever; they both knew the score. And so the cycle recommenced as Eileen and the kids settled down once again to a peaceful life on welfare – saving some of the goodies for Piney's next welcome home party.

CHAPTER FOUR

Tubby's love of food: Country Dance Suppers

It seemed Tubby had an aversion to using an axe, so unless we had a prisoner serving "time" in the lock-up it was Doreen who usually chopped the kitchen firewood. The woodheap was fairly close to our office window and sometimes when we had a visitor in the office, as Doreen started to chop away on the woodheap, Tubby would walk over and pull down the blind saying (with a straight face) "You know I can't stand seeing a woman chop wood."

Although Tubby never drank liquor (neither did I at that time) he smoked rather heavily and suffered occasionally from severe chest infections. He really enjoyed eating and ate like there was no tomorrow. It is not really unkind to say he was "a guts" – he bragged of being so. Doreen liked cooking and was always busy preparing huge quantities of food for Tubby and their two children a boy and a girl, who had inherited not only their father's body shape but also his appetite.

A good example comes to mind. We had just finished morning tea in the Police quarters with Doreen – Tubby having almost single-handedly demolished the batch of hot buttered scones she had prepared – when the subject of hamburgers came up.

Now the preparation and cooking of hamburgers just happens to be one of my fortes. From 1949 until I joined the Police Force in 1952 I had a part-time job at night with the "The Bright Spot" – then a leading hamburger and catering company in Perth – where I rose to the position of a senior hamburger cook. I spoke of my prowess in this field and offered to have Tubby Doreen and the kids to our home one evening for a hamburger meal.

"Mate," said Tubby, "We'd love to come. But there's no way in the world you could cook enough hamburgers to satisfy me and the kids. They love them just about as much as I do."

"Arr .. Harr! .. A challenge!" I replied, "I'll guarantee I'll cook you the best hamburger you'll ever taste, and you and the kids can eat them until they're coming out of your ears if you like!"

"You reckon?"

"I'm sure!"

And so the challenge was mounted. Ample quantities of the required ingredients were obtained (Tubby insisted on contributing to the cost) and the date set. Honour was at stake.

It is important you understand that a hamburger prepared in the original Bright Spot manner is "a real hamburger" – flavoursome and filling – and if you promise not to tell anyone I'll share the secret with you. Okay? Right. Well having prepared your meat balls in advance (good quality mince-meat, pepper/salt and an egg for binding) partially cooked the sliced onions, and finely sliced some lettuce, you start with a slice of lightly buttered toast. The meat ball having been flattened and grilled on a hot plate (or heavy base baking dish) is placed on the toast on a bed of the shredded lettuce. On top of this there is a generous serve of onion (cooked to coincide with meat ball) a splash of Tomato sauce and a lightly grilled egg. Other garnishings such as sliced gherkin, grilled cheese and/or grilled frankfurt can then be added before the remaining slice of toast is placed on top and the hamburger cut in two. One or (at the most) two of my hamburgers is enough for any average appetite.

The battle lines were set: Tubby and his family arrived: the aroma of cooking onions hung in the kitchen air challenging the taste-buds of the contestants. And the cooking began.

Of course, as I knew they would, about an hour later they conceded defeat. In that time Tubby had consumed at least ten hamburgers – that is twenty slices of toast, ten meat balls (500gr), ten eggs, plus onions and other garnishing. His son (aged about 9) had four and his daughter (aged about 6) ate two hamburgers.

*   *   *   *   *

Regular dances and annual balls were a feature of the country social scene in those days. Every few weeks or so a dance would be held at Goomalling or at one of the small out-lying community halls at Jennacubbine or Konnongorring (both of which were in our Police District). They were very popular and and well attended – people came from afar to attend. Of course as farmer's wives are renowned for their cooking, the suppers they prepared for the local dances were superb. Naturally it was part of our responsibility to ensure that these suppers were of the requisite standard. Er... well that was Tubby's "tongue in cheek" explanation why we usually arrived at the venue a dance or two before supper.

Tubby despite his size was fairly light on his feet and enjoyed dancing as much as I did. The ritual we followed when attending one of these out-of-town functions was to park our vehicle as near as possible to the hall – in full view so the "illicit drinkers" would hopefully use their brains and not create a problem while we were about. Then, following a foot circuit of the hall, with a "word" here or there as necessary we would enter the hall, usually having a dance or two (in uniform minus hat) before "checking out" the supper. Oh! ... how well I remember those suppers.

A rather funny thing happened one night as Tubby and I were on our way to a dance at Konnongorring. At

The Konnongorring Hall

The Jennacubbine Hall

48

The popular "Happy Wanderers" Dance Band that serviced the various dances held at Goomalling and surrounding areas in the mid-1950's. Ivy Bullen – violin, Jenny Parker – drums, Jill Parker – saxaphone and Carmel Curley – piano.

that time rabbits were almost in plague proportions. There were hundreds of them on the roads at night and it was impossible to drive anywhere after dark without running over them constantly. This night was no different and we were flattening rabbits galore. When we were about half way there we caught up to a slower moving car. It was after hotel closing time and the vehicle was weaving about on the roadway, so our first thought was that the driver must be drunk. As I drew alongside Tubby called on the driver to stop and he did. Then after I parked my vehicle we walked back to speak to the driver. There were three or four men in the car and the driver got out as we approached.

"What's wrong officer?" he asked.

"Why were you weaving about on the road?" asked Tubby.

"Oh that's all... It's the rabbits" he replied

"The rabbits?" said Tubby "The rabbits? It's a bit damn silly to be trying to run over rabbits"

"What do you mean run'em over? I'm not try'n to run'em over. I'm try'n to save them from bein' run over." the driver replied indignantly. "It's alright for you buggers livin' in town but me and me mates are workin' and livin' at the wheat bin just up the road and hav'ta rely on the rabbits we catch for tucker. So I'm not bloody well goin' to run any over if I can help it!"

It was too much. It was all we could do not to burst out laughing. The bloke was not drunk and seemed to genuinely believe he may jeopardise tomorrow's dinner if he ran over one of the hundreds of rabbits sitting on or crossing the road in front of his car. Controlling his mirth, Tubby sternly warned the driver to steer a straighter course and we left – leaving the man still grumbling to his mates about how little towns-people cared about "us workers livin' it rough in the bush".

CHAPTER FIVE

Guardian Angel or Devil's Grim Reaper

Of course inattentive driving can and often does have serious consequences, particularly in the country where high speed and driver fatigue increase the level of risk, too often resulting in needless loss of life. But then as policemen and other emergency service personnel know too well, you never really know what you are going to find when attending the scene of a traffic accident or any incident for that matter. You may arrive at the scene to find a vehicle or vehicles completely wrecked yet no-one seriously injured, or some dead and others spared. On other occasions there is relatively minor damage, yet death or serious injury has occurred.

There is no doubt in my mind that fact really is stranger than fiction. But whether the Devil looks after his own – saves them or sends his "reaper" to collect his dues – or whether God's "Guardian Angel" protects us from circumstances that should result in death I know not. But I do know there is often no logical explanation for many of the bizarre things I've seen or been involved in as a country policeman. Several such instances come readily to mind.

Late one night Tubby and I were called out to attend a traffic accident involving a tractor and a utility, about midway between Goomalling and Northam. It was reported that persons were injured; the vehicle or vehicles were on fire and a Fire unit was on its way from Northam. Because of the anticipated injuries we drove to the scene in the ambulance. The collision had occurred on an almost straight part of the road in flat claypan country and when we were still at least a mile away we could see the glow of the flames in the sky. Then as we grew closer I saw it was the tractor (a Chamberlain diesel) on fire upside down on the roadway, the gearbox section split open and the engine still running. The tractor and the road surface around it was immersed in a pillar of flame. The other vehicle involved (the utility) was upright partially in the earth drainage channel on the other side of the road, no more than 10 yards from the burning tractor. The utility had severe damage to the front and right side; two injured persons were trapped in the crushed cab; both were conscious.

The acrid smell of hot metal, burning fuel and rubber swirled ominously around the scene. As I ran to the utility the almost over-powering smell of leaking petrol struck me and my senses raced as the injured male driver (who had chest, arm and facial injuries) quickly told me it was high octane racing fuel (aviation grade) spilt from a couple of the four 13 gallon (60 litre) drums he had been carrying in the back of the utility. The fuel drums had split open on impact. He urged us to release his injured wife (suffering from a fractured collar bone and leg injuries) first. There appeared to be fuel everywhere, the vehicle seemed to have been doused in high octane petrol. Even the drainage channel at the side of the road was damp with fuel. It seemed that at any minute there could be one big "whoosh" as the whole lot went up in flames.

Tubby stationed the ambulance well clear. Then using a crowbar to force the jammed doors we released the driver and his wife from the wreckage, and quickly moved them away from the danger area. While we were attending them the Fire Control unit from Northam arrived and started to put out the burning tractor still chugging away upside down on the road. It was a great relief to see those flames go out as it was touch and go for quite a while, as we worked to free the two people from their crushed vehicle. We just had to turn-off and concentrate on what we were doing, as we chatted away to the bloke and his wife trying to reassure them there was little danger. The trouble was the hair on the back of my neck kept going up and down like a damn Venetian blind as the heat of the burning tractor constantly reminded me of the real situation we were in.

Miraculously the tractor driver, apart from being concussed, was otherwise uninjured. He told us he had been driving his new tractor from Perth to his farm North of Dowerin. Shortly before the accident, he stopped to check an unusual noise from the engine, and was actually under the tractor checking a bolt for firmness when the utility struck. He was a Frenchman and I remember him saying "I vos just to put zee spanner on zee nut when boom! zee tractor she go and I am in zee field and my tractor she is split and on fire on the road."

The driver of the utility told us he was returning with his wife to their farm at Cadoux after visiting Perth. Approaching the accident scene on a long slight curve he saw the single white light on the tractor (a light mounted on the rear of tractors to illuminate machinery being pulled at night) and thought it was the headlight of an approaching motorcycle, perhaps a little close to the centre of the road. He didn't have time to brake and struck the tractor at full speed. A car rally enthusiast, he had taken the opportunity while in Perth to purchase the four small drums of high octane racing fuel he was carrying – a decision which almost created a funeral pyre for them both.

Under the circumstances it is really quite remarkable that any of them survived at all. Perhaps God decided it wasn't their time. And while I like to think it WAS God that intervened on this occasion, I also think it may have been that OTHER bloke's hand that saved the life of the villain involved in the following story.

*　　　*　　　*　　　*　　　*

About midnight one night Doreen (Tubby's wife; he again being on sick leave) arrived at my home with a police message that a Holden sedan, stolen from Northam earlier that night, had been seen leaving there about a half hour earlier, travelling north on the Goomalling Road. Donning my usual "turn-out gear" of great-coat slippers, etc., I drove my car to the top of the rise on the main road on the southern outskirts of the Goomalling townsite. Parked about fifty metres up a small track set at a right-angle to the road I had a good overview of any vehicle approaching from Northam. The vehicle I was watching for was a black colour FJ Holden sedan with a Northam registration number. The owner was a Mrs Green, wife of the local Picture Theatre proprietor.

It was a clear moonlit night. Each time I saw the lights of a vehicle approaching from Northam I started the engine of my car ready to give chase, but none of the vehicles passing my concealed observation place matched the description of the stolen vehicle. I must have been there for at least an hour and I was considering giving it away when suddenly a black colour early-model Holden sedan passed before me, travelling in the opposite direction to what I had expected and gathering speed as it left the town boundary heading towards Northam.

It was obviously the stolen vehicle I sought and must have entered Goomalling before I took up my position. As I was unprepared the Holden sedan got away to a good start and apprehension was obviously going to be difficult. Because of the bright moon-light and to preserve the element of surprise I chose to chase after the vehicle without my lights on and soon made up the distance between us. I caught up with the Holden sedan about two kilometres south of Goomalling as the driver took the left fork in the road for Meckering. Both vehicles were then travelling at approx 60 mph (about 100 kph). I switched on my headlights and accelerated to pull alongside of the Holden sedan sounding my horn as a static alarm and crowding the driver in a controlled forced stop manoeuvre.

I had only had my nice new Austin A 50 sedan for about six months at that time, having upgraded from the Austin A 70 utility to accommodate my growing family, and it was my pride and joy. If I had known what was about to happen I think I'd have "had a heart attack".

The thief was taken by surprise. It must have seemed as though my car came from no-where and he started to move his vehicle to the left off the edge of the bitumen on to the shoulder of the road as I pressured him. Then suddenly as he realised what was happening he accelerated and moved the vehicle back again hard against mine, trying to force me back to the right.

It was a crazy dangerous thing to do. The two vehicles were travelling locked together at over 100 kph. He had his front wheels set on a right hand lock keeping his vehicle against me and my wheels were on the opposing left lock, as we both fought for control. For me it was more a matter of self-preservation. I realised that if I braked or moved away, my vehicle would likely roll as soon as the heavy pressure of the other vehicle was released. The whole episode lasted only a few seconds. The Austin A 50 was a very stable vehicle and I had four wheels on the bitumen, whereas the Holden was less stable and had only two wheels on the sealed road and two on the gravel. His nerve cracked before mine and (as I had anticipated) as he braked our vehicles slipped apart and I was forced into a high-speed sliding snaking skid.

Fortunately my vehicle stayed up-right but, as I fought my steering, I could see in my rear-vision mirror the headlights of the stolen car doing a cork-screw roll behind me. As I came to a stop, still facing approximately south, I could see the vehicle still rolling side-over-side along the fence-line behind me. Then it flopped back onto its' wheels and rolled forward onto the bitumen again, coming to a stop facing approximately north-east. The vehicle was quite badly damaged, the driver's door and rear door was open and the driver, apparently injured, was lying half out of his seat almost on the roadway.

Our vehicles were at least 50 metres apart and as I ran awkwardly in my slippers and great-coat towards the damaged car, to my amazement, the young driver (a white male aged about 18) pulled himself back up behind the steering wheel, rammed the engine into gear, and weaved off down the road towards Goomalling trying to slam shut the door as he went. By the time I lumbered back to my car, re-started the engine and turned about to give chase again, I could just make out the tail-lights of the stolen car about a kilometre ahead. Then suddenly the tail-lights disappeared.

Less than a minute later, as I approached a slight left curve on the road about a half a kilometre from Goomalling I could see the lights of a vehicle off the road on the left. It was the stolen car, upright and straddling the remains of the four-strand wire farm boundary fence. The roof of the car had been crushed almost level with the seats and there was other extensive damage to the bodywork; the doors other than the left front door (which was open) were jammed shut; the floor on the driver's side had bulged upwards trapping the shoes of the driver between the brake and clutch pedals, but the driver was not in the vehicle.

I searched the area for quite a while, expecting to find the driver dead or at least seriously injured near-by. From marks on the roadway I could see where the stolen car left the road on the right and rolled over crossing the bitumen surface (probably up-side-down) to finish on top of the broken fence on the other side. In accidents such as this the occupants of the vehicle can be catapulted for some distance clear, so a thorough search was essential. However search as I did, I could not find the young car thief.

What I did find though were the distinct tracks of a person who had run from the scene through the unharvested wheatcrop adjacent to the crash site. I followed these tracks by the light of my torch until they left the wheat paddock and entered a sandy creek bed on the farm. Then retracing my steps I got my car and returned to search along the creek gully for another hour or so. I finally gave up when the foot tracks disappeared as they became mixed in the sandy soil with the tracks of grazing sheep.

So he not only miraculously escaped death but he also escaped capture. My only consolation being that the paddocks the villain passed through in his stockinged feet were riddled with "double-gee" prickles. So by the time he reached home or whereever he came from the car thief must have not only been rather battered and bruised but also very footsore. How anyone could have survived either one of these high speed rollovers let alone two within the space of minutes, without being killed or seriously injured, is astounding. Perhaps the devil really does look after his own.

There is also an unusual but related twist to this story which ought to be told. While I was absent from the accident scene trying to locate the young bloke from the stolen car, then down at the station phoning Northam Police to notify the owner, a resident from Goomalling who was leaving early for Perth, came upon the wrecked car on the outskirts of the town at about 5 am. After searching about and finding no-one he came back to my home, which was about a kilometre away, woke my wife and told her what he had found – a wrecked black colour FJ Holden Sedan with no sign of anyone about. My wife knew the basic details of the stolen car I had gone alone to search for. She mistakenly put two and two together and thought that perhaps I had been overpowered and my vehicle too stolen. She had no telephone to contact the Police station so she asked the man to go on down to the station and wake Tubby. Of course on arriving at the station he found me busily making phone calls and confirmed I knew of the wrecked car.

Because of my involvement I never thought of easing my wife's anxiety by letting her know I was okay. So, by the time I got home at about 6 am, she was in a real mess with worry. Unfortunately we men – particularly those of

57

us who by the nature of our occupation are often exposed to danger – too often over-look the need to ease the anxiety of our loved ones when a phone call or a few minutes away from the job to tell them we're okay, is all it would take. And a final note on this story – surprisingly my Austin A 50 sedan suffered only superficial damage but I did lose a fair bit of rubber from the front tyres. Although the two vehicles were firmly in contact for several seconds there was no actual impact. So closely were they aligned that I had rubber and black paint scuff marks down the entire left side of my vehicle.

*   *   *   *   *

Over the years as I again travel on the Goomalling-Northam Road, and other roads radiating out from Goomalling, I can't help but remember and identify many of the accident scenes I attended over forty years ago and think of those who perished or survived there.

One such place is the junction of the Goomalling-Wongan Hills and Goomalling-Dowerin Roads where, in a car rollover, the young male driver died yet his passenger miraculously survived. The young man who was killed (aged 19) and his brother (aged 18), following in another car, were the sons of a well established local farmer. "Roy" and "John" will do as their names. I knew them both well.

Roy, who was married, was a popular player in the local football competition. He owned a high performance Triumph TR2 red sports car and was known as a bit of a "speedster". During the six months or so before his death I remember serving a couple of traffic summonses on him for speeding offences in the Metropolitan area. His younger brother John also owned a high performance sports car – a dark green Morgan Plus 4. Roy's young wife, expecting the birth of twins, was having problems with her pregnancy and had been admitted to Goomalling Hospital. Apparently Roy and John took the opportunity for a night out together on a driving trip to Perth with a couple of their mates. They both took their cars and each had a passenger.

When they arrived back at Goomalling about daybreak (it was suggested but not confirmed) they decided to race each other back to the farm about twenty kilometres North. Roy, with his passenger asleep beside him in the Triumph, was well in front of John as he approached the "Y" road junction turn-off for Wongan Hills about five kilometres out of Goomalling. The bend itself is a well-banked left curve and I remember being questioned later at the Coronial Inquest as to what speed I thought it could be negotiated safely. I replied that in an emergency I believed I could take the bend, in my medium size family car, with reasonable safety at approx 70 mph (approx 112 kph), and that a high performance sports car, under the control of an experienced driver, should be able to negotiate the bend quite safely at that speed – with a safety ceiling obviously much higher.

Evidence also presented at the Inquest ruled out any mechanical fault in the vehicle, or any suggestion that Roy may have been affected by alcohol at the time. Whether he was weary from his night out and lost control, or whether the vehicle was simply travelling far too fast to take the bend, we'll never know. As the low slung little Triumph sports car left the road, rolling and flipping as it went, Roy died instantly beneath the car when his skull struck the road. Paradoxically Roy's sleeping passenger spilled from the vehicle as it flipped and he was left sitting on the bitumen without a scratch or even a graze on his body. Under the circumstances it is miraculous that he was not injured or killed as well.

Later I discussed the tragic irony of the whole situation with the Doctor, as he conducted an autopsy on the body of Roy, in the small mortuary at the rear of the Goomalling Hospital less than fifty metres from the ward where Roy's pregnant young wife lay. Here we were working to establish the exact cause of death of a young man we both knew well; the husband of the doctor's patient and the father of the un-born twins he was trying to save. And save them he did. Three months later Roy's young widow gave birth to two bonny babies. How sad it is that Roy's love of speed caused his death and that he was not there to share with her in the joy of their arrival.

*   *   *   *   *

When you become familiar with the major causes of road death, then see someone driving (or behaving) in a similar manner, it's not hard to foresee the likely outcome. And when that someone is a friend or person close to you it's very difficult not to comment or worse still, to predict where they are likely to end up. Sadly this is exactly what happened with my friend "Percy" (not his real name).

Genuine friendships don't come easy and for a young cop in a country town you can double the anti. Some people who would befriend you have a hidden agenda and it is not always easy for a policeman to recognize this when working in a small community. As an old-time Irish policeman once said... "To be sure there'd be some that'd kiss yer arse in front of yer face, while they cut yer throat behin' yer back!" He was right of course. So it's really great when you think you've found a true friend you can relax with socially. But what do you do when your friendship and your duty start to conflict? Such was my problem during my first couple of years at Goomalling.

Percy and his wife befriended us soon after we arrived and over a period of several months our families became close friends. Percy was battling to break away from share farming and get started on his own. Like us they had little material possessions but their friendship and hospitality was first rate. We visited them on their farm and they occasionally came for a meal at our home. Our kids got on well together and if they (as a family or Percy on his own) were in town they usually finished up at our place for a meal or a cuppa. I sometimes helped out on my day off with tasks about the farm and Percy also helped me out in gathering and cutting firewood for delivery in his farm-truck to our home. He was a personable man with a ready smile who worked hard and loved socializing. Sadly it was this latter trait that finally affected our friendship as sometimes when Percy came into town he stayed drinking at the Farmers Club or hotel for too long. There was local talk (as there always is) that a few times Percy was quite drunk when he left town to drive home. Once or twice, when he came to our home after he had been "having a couple of beers", he was beginning to show signs that he had drunk a little more than he should – although he certainly wasn't too drunk to drive a vehicle. Even though I valued Percy as a close friend, the time came when I was compelled to say something about the likely result of his drinking. It embarrassed me that I had to.

One night when the two of us were alone shooting rabbits on his farm, I raised my concerns with him. I told him that his drinking appeared to be worsening and there was a strong possibility that unless he heeded my warning, sooner or later I may be forced to arrest him for drunken driving. Percy tried to make a joke of it.

"You're kidding aren't you?" he laughed "Who sez I drink too much I only have a couple when I come in to town."

"That's the trouble Perc," I said. "You don't seem to know when to stop. A couple of times when you've dropped in at home after being at the pub you've been a bit close to the wind. And it worries me that the time may come when I have to arrest you."

"No chance. No chance mate," he jokingly replied, "I never have more than a couple. Don't worry it won't happen."

"I hope you're right," I said, "Because if I have to I will, and, if I do, I hope you'll be man enough for us to remain friends."

I can still see his smiling face now as he laughed again and said, "Hey! Don't be so bloody serious. There's no problem."

But I was very serious as, continuing in the same

vein, I added chillingly "It is serious Perc. And you know what? If I do have to charge you with drunken driving I will probably save your life. For if you continue on as you are, you're going to kill yourself and where's that going to leave your wife and kids?" I obviously didn't get through to him for he laughed again with embarrassment and changed the subject.

Following our "little discussion", over the next few weeks Percy's warm friendship towards me cooled and the relationship between our two families became more of an "at arm's length" casual affair. I was disappointed but not really surprised. Then by some strange quirk of fate my grim prediction became a horrible reality. Percy injured himself while working on the farm (I think he broke his leg or ankle) and had his leg in plaster. A few days later while in Wongan Hills on business he stayed drinking at the Hotel until closing time. And, according to witnesses, he was apparently well "under the weather" when he hobbled out to his truck to drive home. About half-way back to the farm Percy's truck veered slowly to the right. Affected by liquor, he probably lost concentration or dozed off to sleep. It was a fairly straight stretch of road with few trees on the verge, but as the truck left the roadway bouncing on the rough surface it seems Percy's head flopped out of the driver's side window and his skull was crushed by the trunk of a small tree. He died soon after at the Wongan Hills Hospital.

*   *   *   *   *

I will also never forget the circumstances that led to the tragic death of "Les" the pleasant young relief Assistant (railway) Station Master at Goomalling.

Traditionally country policemen tried to meet most of the passenger trains that stopped as they passed through the local station. At Goomalling we usually got to the station early and had a bit of a chat with the Station Master, the Post Master, business people and others waiting for the train's arrival.

On this particular day the conversation centred around the merits of various makes of popular cars. Les, aged about 19, was acting as the relief Station Master that day, and he dominated the discussion with his exaggerated claims about the speed and road holding ability of his relatively new Volkswagon sedan. He bragged about his driving skills and how he kept cutting back on the time it took him to travel to Perth. He even boasted how he had "burnt off" a Council Traffic Inspector late one night as he passed through one of the towns on a run to Perth. I had until then remained a silent observer as others in the group debated and commented on Les's claims. But he attempted to draw me into the conversation as he light-heartedly said "I bet my Volkswagon could out-run your Austin A 50, Bob. Let's have a race around the town block to see which is the fastest."

I could have stopped it right there but I merely said "Don't be stupid."

"Ah come on," he persisted, "It'd be fun. You're the cop. It'd be okay – or are you scared I'd beat you?"

Again perhaps I should have stopped it with a curt remark, but although I quite liked Les, he was beginning to get a little under my skin. So I thought I might "take him down a peg or two".

Foolishly, due perhaps to my own immaturity at the time, I chose to introduce a grisly content to the conversation in an attempt to maybe shock him and encourage him to be less reckless. Shaking my head and assuming a stance of mock exasperation, I said "You young blokes amuse me. How long is it now Les since I gave you your driver's license? About six or seven months isn't it?"

"About nine months actually," he replied.

"That'd be right," I continued, "And here you are going on like you reckon you're Stirling Moss or someone (Stirling Moss being a well known racing driver of the era). If you don't pull your head in Les you're going to have a very nasty accident soon. But, when you do, please try not to involve some other poor bastard. Pick yourself a nice big tree and do a good job of it. There's nothing worse than battling to free a badly mangled accident victim from the wreck of a car while they're still alive, screaming for relief or choking on their last breath, particularly when you know them personally. So do me a favour also and don't have your big prang in my district."

Our small discussion group then broke up as the train arrived. I thought little more about what I said to Les until a couple of weeks later. Then my chilling words came back to haunt me as I learnt he had been killed in the early hours of the morning when his car left the road on the outskirts of the Metropolitan area and struck a tree.

Apparently Les finished work at the Goomalling Railway station at mid-night and set off for Perth in his car. He made it to the top of Greenmount hill in a little over an hour. Some fairly extensive road-works were being done in that locality and there were ample warning signs and lights to alert drivers to the danger. Les either ignored these signs or was unable to reduce speed in time. As he attempted to negotiate a small detour he lost control. His vehicle left the track and collided head-on with the trunk of a large fallen tree. Les died instantly in the wreckage of his beloved Volkswagon fulfilling my grim prediction of such a short time before. And I swore to myself then never again to comment on the likelihood of someone's imminent death, no matter what the circumstances.

CHAPTER SIX

The Rigours of Relief Work

Although the opportunity to relieve as the O.I.C of another station meant a little extra money (because of the allowances) and gave me an opportunity to gain valuable experience, the isolation and loneliness took the edge off any advantage the work offered. When you are sent to a small town as a relief officer you are only really there to maintain the status quo until the local man resumes duty. And when you are stuck there for up to six weeks at a time, missing your wife and kids, often with little work to keep you occupied, it can be very lonely for a young policeman – a factor which often makes him vulnerable to pressures and temptations. And sure there were opportunities and I was tempted. I'd be a fool to suggest otherwise but the moral and ethical standards instilled in me from childhood always came to the fore and saw me through. I never could see any value in jeopardizing my marriage, my self-respect or career by acting contrary to those principles.

I remember arriving in one country town to carry out a period of relief and becoming the subject of unethical pressure from a most unlikely source – a friendly senior justice of the peace. It seems the constable I was relieving was fairly lax and the J.P. thought it would be appropriate to use me to "clean up" some of the locals who regularly

*Bob with his "little kids",
Rodney and Colleen.*

drove their vehicles after having a "few too many" at the
local Farmers Club or Hotel. I had been in the town for
about a week, and after assessing me over a few morning
coffees at his business premises, the J.P. apparently
thought it was time to involve me in his little "plan". He
started by telling me what he thought about people who
drove their vehicles while drunk and I heartily agreed with
him. He then went on to say that nothing was being done
about it in "his" town because the local constable drank
with most of the worst offenders and, that while I was
there, there was an excellent opportunity to clean-up the
problem together. I was surprised as he obviously saw
himself fulfilling a sort of "deputy sheriff" role. And it got
worse: he wanted to supply me with names and vehicle
numbers, and even suggested appropriate times and
places where I could hide in wait for the victims. Of course,
he pointed out, he should be one of the "impartial" justices

who dealt with the matters when brought before Court. I suspect my friendly J.P. may have had a hidden agenda. I heard him out, then assured him that any law-breaker I came across in the normal course of my duty would be properly dealt with. However I told him (as diplomatically as I could) I had no intention of lying in wait for anyone he thought may have had a few too many beers with his mates at the pub. Nice chap really. I wonder what his fellow citizen's would have thought of him had they known of his little scheme?

Because of the position of trust a policeman occupies, he often finds himself in a situation where his integrity is sorely tested. I know. I've been there and on one particular occasion I nearly, or so very nearly yielded. Had I done so my career and self-respect would have certainly been destroyed. How close I came. It still gives me "goose bumps" when I think about it.

I was relieving at Trayning at the time and received a report that a single man at the Main Roads Dept camp a few miles out of town had been found dead in his tent that morning. He had not been attending a doctor and had no history of ill heath. It was one of those routine "sudden death" inquiries where the police, acting on behalf of the Coroner, remove the body, arrange identification and post-mortem, and interview any person who may have relevant information. Where it is not known if the deceased made a "will", or there is no executor or relations to take possession of his belongings, police acting on behalf of the Public Trustee also assist in disposal of the deceased's estate.

In this instance the man who had died was a British citizen who had no known relatives in Australia. Therefore I took possession of all his belongings, which included a car, camping gear, and personal items such as letters and documents. Also, concealed among his property, I found a small tin containing 75 pounds ($150) in cash. Returning to the Police Station I prepared an itemized list of everything collected from the camp and which I was now to hold at the station pending instructions from the Public Trustee. Disposal of the cash found among the deceased's property was another matter. Where actual cash is involved, the money must be banked immediately and brought to account as an amount credited to the Public Trustee.

My wife and I were going through a particularly bad period with our finances where we had to juggle payment of accounts, paying only those which had a dead-line and leaving others for the following month or so. There was barely enough money coming in to meet commitments. The 75 pounds I found in the dead man's property created quite a dilemma. It seemed almost like manna from heaven... or was it hell? My mind was in turmoil. If I took the money who would know? And I would then be able to pay a couple of those worrying accounts (but that would be stealing) No ... not really. Take it, no-one will ever know (but they might) How could they? It was old notes – could have been there for ages (but it's dishonest) Well just take some and bank the rest – no-one will ever know (but—). You're worried about those accounts. You can fix it. You're not actually taking it from anyone. It's a dead man's money. It will only go to the Public Trustee (but — but —).

On and on went my inner turmoil and I'm sure it was "Old Nick" himself urging me to yield to temptation, not to listen to the pleas of my conscience. And he damn near succeeded. Instead of issuing a receipt and banking the money immediately, as I should have done, I left it in my office drawer for a day and a half while the ethical debate raged within me. Finally reason prevailed and I dealt with the cash as I should have done in the first place, including details of the banking with other particulars required for the Public Trustee. Then, when the autopsy report was received from the Doctor a day or so later, showing the cause of death to be "Heart failure", I was able to complete and forward my report to my Regional Officer for consideration by the Coroner.

That should have been the end of it but, almost a fortnight later, the crunch came. Two blokes from the Main

Roads camp came to the Police Station and asked me how they could get their money back.

"What money?" I asked.

"Well we forgot to tell you at the time, what with the shock of him dyin' like he did. The night before he died Syd collected the money from the boys as he always did to pay the grocer bill for the camp. It'd be about 75 pounds we reckon."

Wow! the icicles shot up my spine and it took me a moment or two to recover from the shock of what he had just said. Then, with an inward sigh of relief, I smiled and said, "There's no problem but there may be some delay as I found the 75 pounds among Syd's gear and it's been banked to the credit of the Public Trustee."

It seemed almost as if a breath of cool fresh air uplifted my soul as I handed them a copy of the receipt and told them how to claim their money. How different it all might have been had I risked everything for a lousy 75 pounds. Isn't integrity a wonderful thing?

Of course memories of temptation and pressure are not my only recollections of unusual experiences while relieving at small police stations in the Eastern wheatbelt. Sometimes (rarely would be more correct) the constable I relieved let me use part of his living quarters while he was on holiday. I would then bring my young family with me and, instead of my usual feelings of isolation, the relief period became almost like a holiday away from home.

The nature of my role as the junior policeman at Goomalling often meant that my wife seldom knew what I was doing or what I was involved in, or when to expect me home. On those rare occasions that she was able to come away with me while I was on relief duty she was on the scene – so to speak – and to a certain extent knew what I was doing. For a rather naive young police wife this can sometimes have certain consequences.

I was relieving at Trayning Police station. And as the O.I.C. had allowed me to use part of his quarters, I had my wife and two small children with me. It was really great. There was not a lot of police work to do so much of my time was spent with my family. The Police station and quarters were isolated from the main part of the town by the railway line. It was in the middle of summer and, on the day this little incident occurred, it was as hot as hell – about 116.F (45.C) in the waterbag. Even the crows tried to keep in the shade away from the heat of the mid-day sun. I left the Police station at about 2pm to walk to the Bank, which was in the main area of the town on the other side of the railway line.

Before I got to the Bank a woman, who had been driving by in a farm truck, stopped and asked me for help. She told me that her husband, who was now seated in the passenger seat, was a chronic alcoholic. He no longer cared for himself, had stopped eating and during the past week or so had been drinking methylated spirit. She claimed he was hallucinating and she was terrified what he may do to himself or her in his disturbed state of mind. He had virtually forced her to bring him into town so they could buy more methylated spirit from the general store. She wanted me to stop them from selling it to him.

I explained to her that her husband's problem was really a medical one and that I couldn't legally prevent anyone from selling him methylated spirit, but I suggested we could ask the store manager to co-operate by not doing so. We were close to the store at that time and entered together to speak with the manager. However, before we had a chance, the husband suddenly appeared and violently argued with his wife about involving me. He looked a real mess – like a mad-man about to attack. His bulging blood-shot eyes were almost popping out of his haggard face and his wasted unwashed body shook with tremors. He was beyond rational conversation and suddenly broke away and ran back to the truck, jumped into the driver's seat, started up and drove off down the street to stop and park about 150 yards further on.

I followed on foot and arrested him for driving the vehicle while under the influence of alcohol. It was a convenient way of detaining him until I could sort out the best way to help him overcome the situation created by his drinking problem. He didn't resist me but was very angry with his wife whom he saw as the main cause of all his problems. I took him back to the Police station, charged him and locked him in a cell. Then, as I hadn't yet been to the Bank, I returned almost straight away to the town area. I also needed to discuss my prisoner's problem with the Doctor and arrange a Court so it was about an hour or so before I got back to the Police station. As I entered the yard I was shocked to see my wife leaving the office and walk back towards the police quarters, carrying a large empty jug and a drinking glass.

"What on earth have you been doing?" I asked.

"Oh just giving that poor man in there a drink of water" she calmly replied. "He was so thirsty. He pleaded with me to get him a drink."

"What! You mean you actually opened the cell door to give it to him?"

"Well I had to, and he was just so grateful. He drank the whole jugfull. He's been crying out for a drink of water for ages, and you weren't here to give him one."

"He's dehydrated that's why. The bloke's almost a raving looney. He's been drinking metho for over a week and he's in the rats. I won't even allow him bail because of what he may do to his wife. Do you realize what a risk you took?"

"No I don't suppose I did – I was only thinking about that poor man in there. Surely he wouldn't have hurt me?"

I explained (as gently as I could) that although this particular bloke was not a criminal – more of a victim really – he was mentally disturbed and unpredictable in his present condition. Fortunately, although my precious lady had taken a great risk in opening the cell door as she did, he made no attempt to escape or attack her. She promised me never to enter the lock-up during my absence again.

So what actually became of the metho addict? Well, with the co-operation of the Doctor and the local Justices of the Peace, he was dealt with under the provisions of the (then) Inebriates Act and sentenced to a period of compulsory treatment in a "drying out" facility. I withdrew the traffic charge as he had problems enough as it was. I hope the poor bloke finally overcame his addiction.

* * * * *

Within the first few months of my posting to Goomalling I was sent to relieve the O.I.C. of Toodyay Police station. It was the first time I had run a station completely on my own and, although it was said there was not a lot of actual "police" work at Toodyay, the policeman there also acted as the Clerk of the Local Court, the Clerk of the Licensing Court, Clerk of Petty Sessions, Bailiff of the Local Court, and Registrar of Births Deaths & Marriages. Fortunately most of these extraneous matters were also dealt with at Goomalling so, under my boss Tubby Eaton's tuition, I had a reasonable grasp of the extra duties involved.

Although I was aware I was expected to do little more than keep things going as they were until the other bloke got back from leave, I soon found that my standards and his were poles apart. It seemed he believed that if you did as little as possible (or nothing) you couldn't get into trouble for doing it wrongly. I had a different attitude to my responsibilities so I think the citizens of Toodyay found me a bit of a shock to the system.

I had been there for only a couple of days when a lady came to the station and complained that, a short time before, a box of groceries had been stolen from her car parked in the main street. I took particulars and then spent about a half hour in the area where her car had been parked, interviewing people who may have been in the street about the time the groceries were taken. I learnt that a local man, a middle- aged bloke named "John" (who had seemed a bit "tipsy" at the time) had been seen in the area carrying a box similar to the box said to contain the missing groceries. Sure enough when I went to his house and challenged him, he admitted the offence and I recovered most of the stolen groceries (he was actually preparing a meal with some of them when I arrived). Although John had obviously been drinking, he certainly wasn't drunk and knew what he had done was wrong. I arrested him, took him back to the station, charged him with stealing and placed him in the lock-up.

Feeling rather pleased with myself I returned the remaining grocery items to the lady from whom they were stolen, expecting her to thank me for promptly locating the person responsible. But no. "Oh poor John!" she cried, when I named the thief, "He's such a nice man. He must have really wanted something to eat if he was prepared to steal to get it. I don't want him charged. You'll have to let him go." I explained that you can't simply "un-arrest" someone. It doesn't work that way. John would be brought before the Court on the charge for which he was arrested, and any mitigating circumstances could be explained to the Justices at the time. She was not at all pleased and even returned later with the support of two women friends who also tried to persuade me to drop the charge. They made it quite clear that they thought me to be the "bogey man" and "poor John" the victim. However when John appeared before the Court of Petty Sessions the next morning the Justices clearly understood the real situation. After listening to the facts, and my complainant's pleading on his behalf, they ruled that a blatant stealing offence was not a matter to be taken lightly. They gave John a severe "dressing down" before placing him on a good behaviour bond.

*   *   *   *   *

Although only a small town Toodyay at that time had three hotels, a wine saloon and a licensed club. Those that drank seemed to spread their patronage equally between all licensed premises, moving from one pub to the next as the evening progressed. A bar that had a dozen or so drinkers an hour before was often left deserted a hour later as they moved on. With so much time on my hands I often walked down the main street in the evening – usually in uniform – visiting the various licensed premises and spending a few minutes in each talking with the licensee or bar staff. As you would expect from time to time while taking my "evening stroll" I came across people breaking (or about to break) the law. Depending on the circumstances I had the occasional "word" here and there. Of course this wasn't always appropriate. Like the night I found a bloke urinating on the front door of the Post Office, so "in the bin" he went, charged with committing a nuisance. Although I found (throughout my career) that most people will appreciate the advantage of a warning others sometimes take offence and become indignant about being spoken to.

My decision to have a word with the "President" is a typical example of what I mean. One evening I saw a car parked rather strangely, partly on the footpath, outside the Toodyay Club. It was the only vehicle in that part of the street, yet it had been parked with the left front wheel standing on the footpath about two feet in from the kerb. Entering the Club I could see there were only three people drinking at the bar. Two of them were in casual clothes and the other, a rather portly bloke with a loud voice, was dressed in a suit and wore a tie. I quietly asked the barman if he knew who owned the car outside. He indicated the bloke in the suit and tie.

About this time the big bloke, who was dominating the conversation in the small group, was loudly proclaiming the features of his new car, which he referred to as the "old bus". He was obviously well under the weather so, moving nearer and apologising for interrupting, I introduced myself and asked if he owned the car parked on the footpath outside the Club.

"Yes that's the old bus." He replied.

I told him what I thought about his condition and

warned him not to drive the car again that night, or he may be charged with drunken driving.

"What!" he exclaimed indignantly, "Do you know who I am? I am the President of the ... Branch of the (a prominent political) Party."

Then (as the barman almost choked as he tried to control his amusement) I firmly replied. "It doesn't matter who you are sir. If I find you driving your vehicle again tonight I'll arrest you and charge you with drunken driving."

I suggested he stayed over-night in a hotel or got someone to drive him home. At this he became almost incoherent with anger but his two companions (who seemed quite sober) quickly stepped between us and shepherded him from the bar, telling him to "grab his brains" and heed my warning. The President" wasn't the only local I warned about a possible drunk driving charge during my stay, but he was certainly the most pompous.

*　　*　　*　　*　　*

Unfortunately there are some people who also mistake a warning given politely as a sign of weakness. "Leo the wood- cutter" was one such person.

One evening as I was doing the rounds of the hotels in Toodyay, I entered the Central Hotel at about 8pm. There was only the licensee and one customer in the bar and they were engaged in fairly loud conversation as I entered. I was in uniform and, as I started to walk towards them down the bar, the bloke the licensee was talking to turned his head towards me and said in a loud voice, "I'm not leavin' your f...'n pub and no bloody copper's gunna make me!"

He was dressed in dark clothing, wore a wide-brimmed black hat, and was leaning with both elbows on the bar counter. He appeared much older than me, and as I approached he stood upright and I could see he was about six foot tall (183 cm). I also noticed rather nervously that his well developed chest and arm muscles were almost bursting from his short-sleeve shirt. (I learnt later, he was an axe-man, a contract wood-cutter, so no wonder he had the physique of a weight-lifter)

Addressing the licensee, I said "What's the problem?"

"Oh there's no real problem," he nervously replied "I've just been saying to Leo here that I think he's had enough to drink and should be going home."

Before I could speak "Leo" stepped close to me, clenching his fist and flexing his left biceps muscle under my nose until the material of his shirt sleeve stretched almost to breaking point. He said "Do you want a fight? I'll give you a fight if you want one."

Oh great! I really needed this! To succeed in a physical contest with this bloke seemed like an impossibility. It had to be a battle of wits. I tried to control my racing heartbeat, and avert my eyes from the bulging biceps flexing so close before me, as I said "Are you threatening me?"

"No I'm not threatening you. But if you want a fight I'll give you a fight," he continued, pumping up his damn muscle like a balloon.

I said "Don't be a fool. You've had enough to drink and the Licensee has asked you to leave. If you don't go you'll be charged with refusing to leave licensed premises, and if you keep threatening me like this you'll also be charged with disorderly conduct."

My warning had little effect and he continued with his threatening gestures, and I repeated my warnings about his behaviour, as gradually we moved from the bar onto the footpath outside. But although I had succeeded in getting him out of the pub I couldn't stop his threatening gestures and remarks. I had run out of options. I either had to back down or arrest him for disorderly conduct. Steeling myself in readiness for a struggle I put my hand on his shoulder and said "Right! That's it! You're under arrest for being disorderly and if you resist me you'll also be charged with resisting arrest. Now get in my car!"

To my surprise he didn't resist and meekly got into

76

my car, which was parked at the kerb close by. Although he remained docile as I drove him to the Police station (a small room at the end of the verandah on the Police quarters), I was still fairly nervous when I searched him and recorded his property and personal details in the charge book. But then his attitude suddenly changed as I asked him to come with me across the darkened yard to the cell block. He apparently decided to try to take control of the situation again and he refused to leave the office for the cells until I let him smoke a cigarette. It was a no win situation. If I refused I risked a physical confrontation and if I agreed my level of control could suffer. I capitulated and gave him a cigarette.

Leo made the most of the moment slowly dragging on the cigarette while I stood waiting in silence. Then when several minutes had passed and he was obviously making the cigarette last as long as he possibly could I called a halt, took the cigarette, extinguished it and ordered him to accompany me to the cell block.

All went well until we were almost there. Then he stopped and said he was going no further; that if I wanted him in a cell I would have to try and put him there. And try I did. What a fiasco! It was like dancing with the fat lady in the "square dance". There was the "doe-see-does" and the "swing with ya' partner now" as we grappled and I pushed shoved and swung Leo closer to the lock-up, keeping up a barrage of warnings about what would happen if one of his wild punches actually connected.

I was much nimbler than the drink-affected Leo, and finally managed to get the pair of us into the passage leading to the cells but part of my advantage was lost in the confined space and (reversing roles) he pushed me into a cell and tried to close the door. I had become almost exhausted by then but the thought of facing the embarrassment that would follow if he succeeded in locking me in my own cells spurred me on with renewed vigour. I broke free, swung Leo off balance, and as he stumbled into the open cell I quickly closed and locked the door. He was not at all happy and set about destroying the cell latrine bucket by bashing it against the steel inner surface of the cell door.

The following morning Leo's wife turned up at the station before Court. Now there was a woman. She was taller and heavier than her husband and there seemed not an ounce of fat on her solid frame. Poor Leo the fines and costs the Justices imposed on him for his night on the tiles must have seemed like nothing compared to the "tongue lashing" he got from his spouse before and after the Court as, with bowed head, he followed her home. The Justices explained to me later that Leo's wife ruled the roost. Leo rarely escaped for a night out and when he did he usually got drunk and finished up having a "punch-up" with someone. This was the first time he had been arrested for his misbehaviour.

The narrow passage to the cells where the "Square dance" routine occurred.

The humorous sequel to this story took place about a week later. I was at the barbershop having my hair cut. Seated in the barber's chair with my uniform concealed from view under the protective cover, I was not recognised by the two men who entered and sat down behind me to await their turn. When their conversation turned to "the bloody young copper from Goomalling" the Barber and I exchanged a wink and a grin.

"Who the hell does he think he is

The historic Toodyay Court House built in 1897 and, although rather delapidated, used as a Court until the late 1950's. The building was restored in 1985 and has since been utilised as the offices of the Toodyay Shire.

The old Toodyay Police Lock-up 1860 -1967

anyway?" said one, "Tellin' the fellas they can't drive home after they've had a few beers at the pub. We've always done that in Toodyay."

"Yeah," the other replied "But I wouldna minded bein' there the other night when he told bloody old ... (the President) he'd pinch him if he drove."

The barber (who was enjoying himself) must have decided to stir them up a little, for he joined in adding, "Yeah but he wouldn't take any ... from Leo the other night, would he."

"No. And a bloody good job too," one of them said, "Belted the hell out of him too before he locked him up. Serves him right" (I wondered what they would've thought if they'd known what really happened. How different their story would have been.)

At this the barber, who had finished cutting my hair, pulled the cover off me, brushed me down and said, "Thank you Constable. Call again won't you."

As I turned to leave I smiled and said a "good'ay" to the two (now almost pop-eyed) blokes who had been discussing me so freely.

*   *   *   *   *

During my time as a policeman I never ceased to be amazed at how foolish some people can be. How at times they seem hell-bent on putting themselves in a situation where they're in direct conflict with the law and police, as though they enjoy the blatant challenge. For example: I was relieving at Wyalkatchem while the O.I.C took his holidays and had only been there a couple of days when this incident occurred.

Late one afternoon I was standing in the public bar of the hotel where I was staying with a group that comprised the Licensee and two or three local businessmen. I didn't drink liquor at that time so I had a squash or two as the others drank beer. I was not in full uniform but the clothing I wore more or less identified me as a policeman.

A group of about four other drinkers stood together about fifty feet away around the curve of the bar. They were joking and laughing amongst themselves and seemed to be talking about the group I was in as they frequently looked in our direction. Finally one of them, a fairly tall bloke aged about thirty, moved away from his mates and walked around to stand close behind me. Although he wasn't drunk he was obviously affected by liquor. I turned to face him.

"Good'ay," he said, "Are you the relief cop?"

"Yes I am," I replied, introducing myself asking his name and shaking hands.

"You know what?" he laughed, "Those blokes around there reckon I'm scared of you." Oh God, I thought, here we go.

"Well," I said, "there's no need for anyone to be scared of me so don't take any notice of them."

"Well I'm NOT scared of you," he persisted.

"OK OK OK we both know you're not scared of me." He was beginning to annoy me. "So let's leave it at that. OK?" I said, as I turned back to my group.

"Well I think you're just a bastard!" he came back at me again.

That was it! I'd had enough! Turning back to face him, I said, "You have exactly thirty seconds to apologize for that insult or I'll arrest you."

He didn't reply. He just stood there swaying and grinning. I took his arm and told him he was under arrest, then as he attempted to pull away I applied an arm lock restraint and marched him out to my car which was parked outside. As soon as I arrested him he wanted to apologize, saying it was only a joke, but it was too late. I took him to the Police station and charged him with disorderly conduct, admitting him to bail to appear in Court the following morning. Apparently he wasn't a bad bloke, just a fool who considered himself a comic but he went too far and probably learnt a lesson he never forgot.

*   *   *   *   *

The Hotel at Dowerin was situated directly alongside of the Bank, with the Bank Manager's quarters forming the rear part of the building. I was staying at the Hotel during my period of relief and, as usual, with time on my hands I spent much of my time in the evenings reading by the wood fire on my own in the Hotel licensee's office. Hotel closing time was 9 pm in those days and one night, as I was sitting in the cosy little office reading at about ten minutes past the hour, the telephone rang. It was customary for me to answer any incoming calls if I was there on my own (sometimes the call was for me) so I picked up the telephone and, without identifying myself, I simply said, "Hello"

The caller said, "Oh Jack (the licensee's name) it's Charlie (the Bank Manager) Do me a special favour will you and pass me a half dozen cold bottles of beer over the side fence. Some friends of ours have arrived unexpectedly from Perth and I haven't got a drink in the house. I'll fix you up for them tomorrow, but watch out for the young copper from Goomalling won't you."

Oh nice one Charlie, I thought, what the hell am I supposed to do or say now. Well ... under the circumstances it seemed unlikely the world would end if I turned a blind eye to a minor breach of the Liquor Licensing laws, so I just said, "Ok", and put down the phone.

I explained what happened to Licensee Jack and urged him not to embarrass the Bank Manager by revealing who he had actually spoken to on the telephone when arranging his little "illicit" deal. However I suspect he did for, although nothing was said about the over-the-fence arrangement, poor Charlie was obviously most uncomfortable when we next met.

CHAPTER SEVEN

Crop Fires and other Events

Friday afternoon at Goomalling was the day when most farmers found an excuse to come into town for business or just to socialize. It was also an opportune time for us (the police) to catch up with people from the outlying areas who we needed to speak to about various matters. Friday afternoon was one of our busiest times. If not in the office we would be walking down the main street (often together) doing a bit of socializing ourselves.

Tubby was quite a character and always had a good yarn to spin. Often when we were in a group he would turn to me after telling some outrageous story (usually one I'd never heard before) and say, "That's right. Isn't it Bob?" While personally I was thinking "what a whopper" I'd pull myself back from my private thoughts and of course reply, "Yes... Yes..." (dared I differ?)

Like any farming community the farmers at Goomalling were very close-knit and supportive of each other, particularly in times of ill-health and hardship. I vividly recall the many busy-bees to help plant or harvest the crop of a farmer (or widow) who because of some unforeseen reason was unable to do the job himself. The same applied when there was a crop fire. In those days the railway trains were mainly coal-fired and during the summer months many crop fires were caused by sparks from passing trains. The wheat crops were tinder-dry and ready for harvesting at that time, and a severe crop-fire could wipe-out a whole season's work, often affecting more than one property as it quickly spread. So during the critical time before harvesting, farmers and townspeople alike nervously watched the sky. At the first sign of smoke or other warning everyone dropped whatever they were doing and turned out to assist. All farms and local councils kept a truck utility or heavy trailer on stand-by as a ready-to-go fire-fighting unit.

A turn-out to a crop fire was something to see. In such an emergency fences gates and other obstructions were often ignored as vehicles raced by the shortest route to the seat of the fire. Unbelievable risks were taken by some as they desperately sought to stop the fire. I remember Gerry Lockyer ("The Beard") – whose farm adjoining the railway line was often one of the most affected – driving his old utility down the tongue of the racing fire as it advanced through his crop. Steering with one hand, his head and shoulders out of the cab so he could see through the smoke and flames, the Beard was directing water from the hose attached to the fire unit he was towing, desperately attacking the fire from the rear as he followed only a few yards behind. Other units, with men using water hoses and running beside, attacked the fire on its flanks and it was brought under control. The Beard had an unscheduled beard trim (singeing) but it could have been so much worse.

*   *   *   *   *

Football and farm problems were generally the topic of most Friday afternoon group conversations/ discussions. There was often talk or rumours about sheep stealing activity and while there probably was (and still are) genuine instances of stock theft, we found that most stock losses were due to bad management: some even falsely reported as theft. I remember where in one case our inquiries showed that the cocky concerned clearly neglected his sheep, which were heavily mortgaged to a stock firm, and as a result many died. He attempted to conceal the carcases and reported the loss as a theft not realizing how thoroughly police would investigate the matter. Although we found insufficient evidence to charge him with fraud, we certainly showed him up for the fool that he was.

The investigation of stock theft is always tedious and often back-breaking work. Invariably most of these "alleged" thefts seemed to occur in summer. It was hot and dirty work. While I am sure most complainant's initially believed their sheep had been stolen, in most instances we found the loss was due to their own neglect, either through faulty counting, incorrect recording, poor fencing, deaths (lack of feed/water) or fraud.

I will never forget the first such investigation that I did on my own. It was within the first 18 months of my posting to Goomalling and, as I set off in my car at day-break, I didn't feel very confident about my chances of success.

I turned off the Jennacubbine Road onto the farm and, as I got out of my car to open and close the gate to the home paddock, I saw them sitting on the top rail of the stock yards near the shearing shed, about a hundred metres from the house. As I drew up and stepped from my car I got a closer look at the three men waiting for me. One was about forty five years of age and the others only slightly younger. They were lean weather-beaten tough looking blokes, dressed similarly in work worn shirts and jeans, high heeled riding boots (one had spurs) and battered bush hats. Close by two saddled horses were tied to the back of a horse-float. I felt as though I had stumbled un-invited onto the set of a "Western" movie – just as the cameras were about to roll.

I too, with my contrasting appearance was clearly not what they had expected. Their body language said it all. I was only half their age; wearing my Police issue white

"Pith" helmet, old issue navy blue serge trousers and long sleeve blue Police shirt – clothing no longer suitable for general use, but ideal for the job at hand. To these blokes I must have looked like the classical "rookie" straight from training school.

As I stepped forward and introduced myself the senior member of the group (who was in the process of rolling himself a cigarette) paused in his task and looked sideways at his companions shaking his head as though in disbelief, leaving me standing there like a "shag on a rock" as I waited for him to respond. Then, slowly transferring his "makings" to the cigarette paper he had been holding on his bottom lip, he accepted my outstretched hand and said, "So you're gunna find the bloke that pinched our sheep are ya?"

It is too long ago now to remember his name, let's say it was "Charlie". He didn't bother to introduce his companions, but un-smiling they each accepted the handshake I offered with little more than a grunt. I felt more than a little intimidated by their attitude. It wasn't a good start and I silently cursed my boss Tubby Eaton for sending me out to do the inquiry on my own. This wasn't the first sheep stealing inquiry I had been involved in. There had been several other reports of "alleged" sheep theft within our Police District during the previous year or so but, until then, Tubby and I had always investigated them together. It was always a mongrel of a job, usually taking at least a week or two of painstaking investigation. Checking records, boundary fences, wool brands and/or ear marks, mustering and counting sheep and questioning neighbours and the complainant alike, to confirm or reject information. As with any investigation, nothing is taken for granted or assumed correct without supporting evidence. Seldom if ever was a report of alleged stock theft made by an efficient farmer. It was always the bloke with the "She'll be right" attitude.

I remember well one of the first such inquiries Tubby and I did together. The complaint had come from "Old

Mick" the senior member of a well known (but then very casual) local farming family. Mick said they had mustered all the sheep on their Konnongorring property (north of Goomalling) a few days earlier, and found about two hundred missing – compared with a count made a few weeks before. There was the usual rumour about a stock truck seen in the area late at night without lights, which Mick was sure must have been involved.

Arrangements were made and we arrived at the property soon after dawn. The sheep had been mustered the previous day and were held in the stock pens adjacent to the shearing shed. Even back in the 1950's farmers were required by law to identify their sheep by both a registered wool brand, and a registered ear mark. The same applies to this day, but now in addition all sheep must also be identifiable by a coloured plastic ear tag, embossed with the owner's brand. An efficient farmer usually re-brands his sheep with the painted wool brand whenever the opportunity arises, such as at crutching time, to ensure the brand remains legible as the wool grows. The "she'll be right" bloke rarely bothers.

Examination of "Old Mick's" penned sheep failed to show any sign of a legible wool brand, and the ear marks were likewise un-identifiable. Tubby Eaton asked to examine Mick's ear marking pliers, to help with identifying the ear mark. Ear marking pliers are designed to act like a punch, removing a portion of the animal's ear in a pattern (and location) registered with the Department of Agriculture. Tubby's request for the ear marking pliers at first met with an embarrassed silence.

"So what about the pliers, Mick?" Tubby repeated.

"Well err, bit of a problem there." Mick drawled, "You see a couple of years back I dropped them, and the bloody thing broke. Since then I've been nippin' a bit out'a the back of their ear with the hand shears!"

So the checking and counting began, and although the numbers were similar to Mick's count, it was almost impossible to establish clearly which sheep were his, for we also found sheep with the ear marks of at least two adjoining neighbours and it's not hard to imagine the difficulty created by Mick having "nipped a bit out with the hand shears" over the past couple of years. It didn't get any better as the inquiry went on, for we not only found the boundary fences to be in poor condition, there was clear evidence that stock had been passing back and forth for some time. This was confirmed when we found many of Mick's sheep mixed with sheep on adjoining properties. So how could Mick and/or his neighbours have really known (with any accuracy) how many sheep they owned at any time? It was a real mess.

After several days of back breaking work we failed to find evidence to support the suggestion that any of Mick's sheep had been stolen, and he (pardon the pun) sheepishly agreed.

Before getting on with the current story, there's another typical incident I'd like to relate which emphasizes the lackadaisical manner in which some farmers record(ed) stock numbers. Soon after our arrival on the farm concerned, we asked the farmer for details of his last stock count. Then we watched in disbelief as the bloke started to search along the wall of the shearing shed, brushing the dust away from the corrugated iron wall sheets as he went.

"What are you doing?" asked Tubby.

"Trying to find the stock figures," replied the farmer, "I'm sure I scratched them on the wall with a nail, somewhere about here after last shearing."

Great start. And the rest of the inquiry went the same way.

Anyway old Tubby was a good teacher and I a conscientious learner. When we worked together there was never any doubt who was the "lacky" and who supervised. He taught me well and always made sure the job was done thoroughly. When the phone call came the day before, reporting the theft, he obviously thought it was time I handled such an inquiry without the benefit of his supervision. So here I was, tackling my first sheep stealing inquiry alone with three less than friendly (apparently experienced) older men to assist me.

The property was owned and operated by a widowed lady, assisted by her brother Charlie. Apparently the stock company Elders GM had an interest in the sheep on the property and had been monitoring them over a period of time. A recent muster and check of numbers, disclosed a discrepancy of 300 on a count made three months previously. Both musters had involved Charlie, the "boys", and the stock agents.

I explained to Charlie the procedure Police followed when making such inquiries. My first move was to confirm figures by an examination of the stock records. I found that most details – such as dates, numbers and other data – seemed to have been correctly recorded, but it was necessary to make adjustments to some figures to allow for deaths, births and killers (ie. sheep killed for home consumption). Of course Charlie couldn't see the point of wasting time on "all this academic bull" when I should be out trying to find out more about "a semi-trailer stock truck that someone had seen late at night near the back property". (You know the "phantom stock truck" that was always about). To say that Charlie had "a chip on his shoulder" would be putting it mildly – it was a railway sleeper – and our relationship got worse as the morning wore on.

After examining the records and making necessary minor adjustments I confirmed that a large number of sheep were unaccounted for, close to the 300 reported. The next step being an examination of the property, I asked Charlie to draw me a "mud map" indicating roads, features and paddocks. This he did, explaining that there were 1200 acres in the home property paddocks and 5000 acres of semi-cleared sand plain country in the back paddocks, about five miles north. He suggested that we ignore the home paddocks as stock numbers had been correct there, and concentrate on the sand plain, as this was where the numbers were down and (of course) that's where the semi was seen.

"And I hope you can ride a bloody horse if you're gunna' check out there," he added with a smirk, "The sand is that bloody loose you can't drive a vehicle around in it. Me and me mates have been riding our bums off out there for the past week, and they're gone for sure. You'd be wasting your time, I'm tellin' ya! "

Oh great! He sounded pretty convincing, and I shuddered when I thought of trying to ride a horse for the first time in my life. But my limited investigative experience made me cautious about ignoring possibilities other than the obvious. So I decided to give the home property the full treatment first, despite Charlie's attitude.

Back to the mud-map, and more detail extracted from an almost hostile Charlie. I noted that the home property was to the South of the east/west Goomalling Toodyay Road, and was in turn dissected almost at right angles by the Jennacubbine Bolgart Road. The homestead, shearing shed and some paddocks were on the west side of this road, and the remainder on the other. There was a fair bit of un-cleared land in this latter part and a small creek bed traversed it North to South.

With Charlie driving a small ex-army jeep, I insisted we criss-cross the paddocks near the homestead first. I counted the sheep carcases we found and checked the boundary fences for security, sometimes walking down to check an inaccessible corner whilst Charlie sat fuming in the vehicle. Then moving to the paddocks on the other side of the road, I did the same. I found that where the creek bed passed through a fence-line, several "creek crossings" (a series of light fence posts unfixed but supported on fencing wire, designed to stay upright and rise with the water level) were lying flat. Heavy traffic in sheep tracks, showed that sheep regularly moved unrestricted along the creek bed.

Some of the paddocks had recently been harvested, and among the stubble or in the un-cleared scrub areas we located small bunches of sheep, some in groups of as many as forty or fifty.

Using Charlie's two companions (who had been left sulking near the shearing shed) I co-ordinated a thorough muster of sheep in the eastern paddocks of the home property. I drove the jeep, Charlie had a motor bike and his two mates were on horseback. We started at the eastern boundary fence and moved westward in a rough line, ensuring that no sheep avoided the muster as we drove them up to the pens adjacent to the shearing shed on the other side of the road.

It was soon obvious we had mustered far more sheep than (a now somewhat subdued) Charlie and the boys expected, and Charlie was all for doing the count himself. But by now I really "had my tail in the air" and insisted on doing the count myself, as the others let the sheep through one at a time at a pace I could handle. As the figures rose well past the number of sheep counted by the Stock agents and Charlie a week or so before, the missing 300 were soon accounted for. Poor Charlie simply didn't know what to say. He could not understand how the error had been made, but the total figures spoke for themselves, clearly no sheep had been stolen. He couldn't apologize enough. Obviously, somehow sheep numbers had been mixed up and/or the muster had not been properly done. The contrast between Charlie and his mates' disdainful attitude towards me when I came to the farm, and their almost fawning apologies as I left, gave me much satisfaction.

But then I too had experienced a change in attitude. Whereas I arrived on the farm at about five that morning more than a little nervous and resentful at having to face what appeared to be a huge task alone, I was back at Goomalling enjoying morning tea with Tubby by 10am, my confidence high and expressing gratitude for the chance he had given me to establish my credibility as an investigator.

CHAPTER EIGHT

The Goomalling Ambulance.

During the early period of my service at Goomalling the town had no ambulance and, in an emergency, had to rely on the availability of an ambulance from either Northam or Wongan Hills. As was frequently the case (particularly in serious traffic accidents) we couldn't wait for an ambulance, and transported the injured by whatever means available. I don't think we even had a basic field stretcher, as I vividly recall using the removable top of the Hospital operating theatre table to move a critically injured railway accident victim to Hospital in the back of my utility. Apathy reigned until the tragic death of a young mother and her unborn child in a traffic accident close to town in March 1955. Her death became the catalyst we used to get the Goomalling people involved.

I attended many serious traffic accidents and dealt with much death during my service as a policeman, but the horror associated with the death of this young woman is something I will never forget. Their names don't matter, lets say it was "Jack" and "Mary".

It was about nine o-clock on a mild Autumn morning early in March 1955, when they left Northam to drive to Wongan Hills. Jack was really looking forward to taking up his new position as a farm labourer on a property North of Wongan Hills and chattered away to Mary and the kids as they motored along the Goomalling Road with their few possessions in the back of the old Ford V8 ute – which he'd purchased second hand the week before on the strength of his new job.

Mary, in the ninth month of her pregnancy, was concerned that the eldest of her two sons aged 8 years would settle down in the new school. But Jack was more concerned about the calibre of the Doctor at Wongan Hills and (of equal importance) whether he would be on hand when their third child arrived in a few weeks time. It was a bit crammed in the front of the ute with Mary's size and the two boys squirming about squabbling over the seat by the window. Jack kept at them to "watch out for Mum" – alternating his attention between what they were doing and the road ahead.

When they were about one and a half kilometres south of Goomalling, just past the old turn-off for the Meckering Road on the down-hill gradient, Jack's attention relaxed momentarily and he allowed the left hand side wheels of the ute to drift off the bitumen onto the broken shoulder of the road. They weren't travelling fast and he probably could have simply steered back onto the bitumen with little if any trouble but being unfamiliar with the vehicle he immediately applied the foot-brake – hard!

In the 1950's many vehicles on the road had the old type mechanical brakes that operated fixed rods when the brakes were applied. Jack's old Ford V8 ute was one such vehicle. But worse still, unbeknown to Jack, the previous owner had stupidly disconnected the left front brake rod because of a fault – tying the loose rod back to the chassis with a strip of canvas to stop it falling to the ground. So as Jack applied the foot brake sharply, the left front brake didn't work but the one on the right gripped firmly causing the vehicle to swerve hard right and before he could make a correction he lost control. The utility left the road sliding sideways flipped over and rolled several times, strewing people and possessions over the area. As the vehicle flipped end-for-end Mary was apparently catapulted through the windscreen onto the bitumen, suffering severe head and internal injuries. Miraculously neither Jack nor the boys were hurt.

A passing motorist was on the scene within minutes and continued on to Goomalling to summon Police help. My quick phone calls established that the Doctor was temporarily out of town and the Northam Ambulance was on its way to Perth with a patient. It was left to us with our limited resources and First Aid training to do what we could. A quick examination of Mary at the scene showed me that her injuries were obviously critical. Her husband and two children appeared unhurt. I felt so helpless. I had an unconscious pregnant woman bleeding freely from massive head injuries, tossing about on the roadway. I cleared her air passages as best I could and tried to check for broken limbs but any thorough examination was virtually impossible. She urgently required skilled medical care and had to be taken to Hospital immediately. We placed a single mattress, thrown from their ute, alongside Mary, lifted her onto this then placed both her and the mattress on the back of my Austin A 70 utility.

I dealt with many shocking situations in almost 36 years as a policeman but that scene still impacts on me now – the total situation; the stark horror in the eyes of Jack as he stood frozen in disbelief with his two little kids beside him helplessly watching as I wrestled with the blooded form of his dying wife, desperately trying to keep her on the back of the utility as I appealed for someone in the crowd of onlookers to help me. Only one person, an elderly man, responded and clambered up to help me restrain Mary on the back of the utility as Tubby drove us to the Hospital.

Sadly Mary died, and efforts at the Hospital to save her un-born child were likewise unsuccessful. All that could have been done was done and it was never suggested that the presence of an ambulance may have made any difference.

The tragedy prompted discussion within the community about the need for a local ambulance service but, as is so often the case, while people generally thought it was a good idea not too many were initially prepared to do anything about it. In fact when the local newspaper published an article calling for a public meeting to discuss ways and means of obtaining an ambulance for Goomalling only four persons attended – we two policemen, the Shire Clerk Frank Coate and the newspaper Editor Geof Ferguson. Disgusted Tubby and I returned to the Police station and, over a cuppa, considered what else we could do. It was Tubby's idea – I remember well him saying "We need to put them on the spot; to make them too embarrassed not to attend." It was a great idea and we applied it as follows.

First we carefully listed the names of business people and other prominent citizens who we thought could make a valuable contribution. The venue for the meeting was re-booked for the following week and we drafted a statement along these lines to head up our list of "nominees".

"Because of public apathy, a meeting scheduled for (time/date) in the Lesser Hall Goomalling to discuss the purchase of an ambulance to service this district failed through lack of attendance.

We believe the need is urgent and that we must get together and start fund raising as soon as possible.

The Hall has been re-booked for Thursday next at 7.30pm. The meeting will be a success only if we have your support.

Please sign against your name and indicate (yes or no) whether you share our concern and will attend this vital public meeting".

Each person listed was then personally presented with this ultimatum and given the opportunity to indicate themselves as a concerned citizen or – by indicating "no" – acknowledging they didn't care.

Tubby was right. The desired effect was obtained.

When the meeting of our nominee group was held in the Goomalling Lesser Town Hall on April 3, 1955, 35 people attended and they unanimously decided to form a St John Ambulance Sub-Centre and commence fund raising forthwith.

The old axiom that if you want a task done quickly, then get a busy man to do it, proved very true for most of the committee, in spite of heavy business or personal commitments, threw themselves almost totally into the task of fund-raising. The problem was dealt with like a crack military operation. The district was divided, targeting groups of people to be canvassed by collectors – each armed with blank cheques, procuration orders and receipt books. The theme adopted was "If everyone donates as much as they can afford, we will succeed". Collectors (mainly members of the committee) made much use of the tragic circumstances of Mary's death – pointing out that although the presence of an ambulance may not have saved her life, at least she could have been dealt with with more dignity. When the right stimulus is provided and a group of positive people can be brought together with a common objective, wondrous things can be made to happen. Such was the case with our fund-raising drive, for within five days 2,054 pounds (including a lottery grant of 500 pounds) had been collected and the ambulance ordered.

The pace continued and the Ambulance – a modified Dodge van – was delivered on June 3, 1955 exactly two months after our successful first meeting. On that day also the new ambulance was dedicated at a public ceremony held in Anstey Park Goomalling involving ministers of the Church of England, Catholic Church and Methodist Church. The spirit of the St John Ambulance movement in Goomalling at that time was so positive and on-going support so strong, that the Committee instituted a bold move to provide an ambulance service free of charge to the patient, regardless of distance or place of residence – reliance being placed on regular donations and fund raising activities. The provision of a "free" ambulance service was quite unique and (I believe) remained in operation as such for at least ten years.

Then, as we had no Sub-Centre building, fund raising activities were directed to target this need and to provide equipment for the van. The ambulance being temporarily garaged at the Police station in the old stables. Classes in First Aid training were also commenced (with the Assistance of the Northam St John Ambulance Brigade) and by October 1955 the Goomalling Brigade became operational. The enthusiasm was infectious, it seemed almost everyone wanted to help in some way with fund raising. We had a small area of wheat planted as a share-farming project; there was a "black wool" drive (most farmers had a very small quantity of natural black wool from their flock, which when combined into one lot could fetch a good price) and a bottle and battery drive. Our most successful on-going fund raising vehicle was the chocolate wheel. Manned by members of the Brigade and other volunteers our chocolate wheel stall with a range of quality merchandise for prizes, was always well patronized at Country shows and other similar events.

In February 1956 a plan for the Ambulance Sub-Centre building was adopted; land in Forrest Street opposite the Goomalling District Hospital purchased, and a tender for the construction of the building accepted. To save on costs, the delivery of the bricks required for the building was arranged with the assistance of local farmers. Ten volunteer farmers took their trucks to the brick works in Perth and by special permission of the Transport Board, returned in convoy to Goomalling where a team of volunteers unloaded the bricks by hand onto the building site.

The official opening of the Goomalling St John Ambulance Sub-Centre on November 24, 1956 – with the ambulance and building paid for and a fully qualified St

John Ambulance Brigade servicing the district all within the space of 19 months – is a tribute to the people of Goomalling and the spirit of the St John Ambulance movement in particular.

*   *   *   *   *

There is seldom much humour in transporting injured people and patients by ambulance but one such instance I do remember was a time when Syd Anderson (our local Dentist and a qualified Brigade member) and I attended a traffic accident at Jennacubbine. Three people had been injured, two of them quite seriously and the third had a broken collar bone. On the return trip to Goomalling I was driving the ambulance with the bloke who had the broken collar bone (arm in sling) seated beside me. Syd was in the back attending the two stretcher cases.

We had only been travelling for about 15 minutes when my patient who was in shock, told me he was about to pass out. "Hold on", I told him as I stopped the ambulance, "I'll get something to help you." I ran to the back of the ambulance, opened the doors and asked Syd to pass me the bottle of Sal Volatile (a liquid aid in the treatment of shock) a medicine glass and water for my patient. He was pretty busy with his two patients and I had to wait a bit before he could do as I asked. Then he passed me the small bottle from the First Aid kit, the medicine glass and a bottle of water. I measured out the required quantity; topped up the medicine glass with water; opened the passenger side door; propped up my now almost unconscious patient and urged him to drink. Down the hatch it went, then... "Phew...!" he gasped, exhaling in my face as the raw spirit sank home.

"God! that tastes like methylated spirit."

"Yeah I suppose it does," I quickly replied, as my senses reacted to the pungent smell and I realised I had indeed given him methylated spirit. You see the First Aid kit carried in the ambulance contained six identical small

A group of the inaugural Goomalling St John Ambulance Brigade, led by "Tubby" Eaton. Photo taken at a Special Parade held at Perth Oval on 14th April 1956 for review by the visiting Superintendent in Chief – Countess Mountbatten of Burma.

The Goomalling St John Ambulance Sub-Centre Building 1997 – opened 24th November 1956.

A group of Goomalling St John Ambulance Brigade Cadets, with Cadet Leader Neville French. Photo taken at the inaugural Cadet Day held on Perth Esplanade on October 13th 1957 for review by Sir Charles Gairdner, Knight Commander of the Order of St John.

brown bottles – each filled and labelled with a different liquid. Syd who was under stress dealing with his own two patients passed me what he thought was the Sal Volatile and I likewise didn't notice it was the bottle containing methylated spirit. Still the teaspoonful of meth. my patient induced wouldn't have harmed him. In fact he brightened up considerably and was quite perky by the time we got to the Hospital – commending me on how good our "Sal Volatile" was.

* * * * *

As you would expect there were many life and death dramas involved with the ambulance service which are not suitable for re-telling, but the incredible luck associated with this particular incident warrants its inclusion.

It happened about six months after we purchased the ambulance. A baby born with a heart defect – a "blue baby" as they were then known – had to be taken by ambulance to Princess Margaret Hospital as an emergency transfer. I was the driver and a sister from Goomalling Hospital travelled with the critically ill baby.

As it was to be a "high speed" transfer, Traffic Patrol in Perth arranged for a Police motor cycle patrolman to meet the ambulance near the foot of Greenmount Hill on the outskirts of the city and escort us to Princess Margaret Hospital in Subiaco. The highways in the 1950's were not of the standard they are today but our modified Dodge Van ambulance had excellent road holding capability and I made it to Greenmount in an hour and a half – averaging better than 60 mph (just under 100 kph) – to meet up with the Police escort. Ideally an escort should allow the ambulance to set the pace, keeping sufficiently in front to allow for emergency braking. If the escort is too close he could be run down and if he's too far in front, other traffic is inclined to squeeze back in between the escort and the ambulance. My escort on this occasion was obviously unaware of the importance of these rules.

We were travelling in the vicinity of 100 kph when the Patrolman picked us up at the bottom of Greenmount Hill, and commenced the escort along Great Eastern Highway Midvale. But instead of allowing me to maintain my speed and set the pace (which was pretty damm dangerous as it was), he took off signalling me to follow and was soon leaving the ambulance behind. I initially increased speed attempting to keep up with him, but because of the widening gap I was forced to travel to the incorrect side of the road as some vehicles moved back between us. It was far too dangerous as I was by then travelling at well over 100 kph on the wrong side of the road and traffic was becoming congested. So after a short distance I aborted the escort by removing my foot from the accelerator to allow the reduced engine power to slow the ambulance but, as I did so, there was heavy vibration and suddenly all hell broke loose. There was a loud banging clanging noise; the cab quickly filled with smoke and petrol fumes and the back of the ambulance bucked and jolted lurching from side to side as I fought for control.

I had no idea what was happening. I thought I may have lost a wheel or wheels. My main concern was fire so I switched off the ignition (in those days there was no power steering or steering lock) and concentrated on steering without touching the brakes. A guardian angel must have been watching over us as the ambulance remained upright and didn't catch fire, gradually slowing to a grinding halt with petrol spewing from its fractured tank. I quickly helped the very shaken but uninjured nursing sister and baby out of the back and clear of the ambulance, and they continued without delay in a Taxi to Princess Margaret Hospital – escorted by the Police patrolman who had returned to assist us.

Examination of the ambulance at the scene and later at the repair workshop showed that when the van was originally modified and lengthened as an ambulance, the tail-shaft had also been cut and extended. The extended tail-shaft was either slightly out of balance or there was a fault in the welded joint. As the full thrust of the ambulance's deceleration was suddenly applied the tail-shaft could not take the additional stress and broke in two. The flailing parts slashed through the fuel tank and brakes lines and severely damaged the floor. The broken rear section still attached to the differential spiked the roadway creating a "pole vaulting" effect. Miraculously my instinctive action in switching off the engine ignition stopped the other end of the tail-shaft attached to the gear-box from continuing its destruction of the floor in the back of the ambulance and further endangering the nursing sister and our small patient inside. It was a very frightening experience. That we survived at all was a miracle in which surely God and Saint John had a hand.

*   *   *   *   *

As time went on I seemed to become almost totally immersed in Ambulance matters at Goomalling. What with on-going fund-raising activities, First Aid training classes, Brigade commitments and normal police duties, in retrospect I believe I may have unwittingly neglected my wife and children. For precious time that I should have spent with them was spent in other albeit worth-while directions.

By February 1958 my interest started to wane. Tubby received his promotion to the rank of Sergeant and no matter how I tried I couldn't get his replacement Constable Bob Gilchrist involved – not that I blamed him. While Bob didn't mind me devoting so much of my own time and the department's time to Ambulance activities, he wasn't interested in doing the same. Anyway the Sub-centre and Brigade were well established by then and the urgency for his involvement no longer existed.

As one of the principal initiators and long term fund-raisers I became particularly frustrated as other "workers" on the Committee progressively dropped out to be replaced by "prestige seekers". I then had difficulty in getting the Committee to approve or upgrade essential equipment needed for the Ambulance. The finance was there but they were reluctant to let me spend it for the purposes for which it had been raised. By mid-1959 I'd had enough and resigned from the Committee – retaining my involvement with the Brigade and Ist Aid classes only.

An abridged version of this episode was published in the Avon Valley Advocate on February 3rd 1998.

103

CHAPTER NINE

Beekay

In country centres Justices of the Peace are an integral part of the judicial system. In the absence of a Magistrate they are regularly called upon to decide the guilt or otherwise of persons charged by the police and brought for trial before the Court of Petty Sessions. They should to be persons of the highest integrity whom the community can rely upon to act without fear or favour; to "do the right thing" at all times. But despite the screening process before their appointment, like policemen, there are some who would use or attempt to use their position corruptly. The power and influence a Justice of the Peace holds because of his position can be quite intimidating. I know because that was the position I found myself in when I refused to forego what I saw as my duty.

"I'm tellin' you if you don't withdraw this bloody summons, by the time I'm finished with you they'll run you out of town on a greasy pole!" He snarled.

Wow! This wasn't some yah-hoo speaking. This was my good friend Beekay – leading business-man and respected senior Justice of the Peace – demanding that I withdraw a traffic summons I had issued against Beekay junior his 18 year old son.

However Beekay's hostility was not entirely unexpected. The warning signs were clearly there when I spoke to him a month or two earlier about a border-line breach of the Prevention of Cruelty to Animals Act committed by young Beekay. I had already warned the teenager about his behaviour but he made it obvious he thought my warning a joke – it wasn't. So in view of his father's high profile as a Justice of the Peace, I decided to discuss the matter with him. But, instead of supporting me as I expected, Beekay was very annoyed that I should even consider questioning "his" son's conduct. I knew he doted on the teenager, a pleasant enough young man (with an over-indulgent father) who simply needed a bit of discipline, but in view of Beekay's Court experience I hadn't expected him to be so strongly biased. However the particular matter was not serious enough to pursue, so I suffered a minor "lecture" from Beekay and took it no further.

Before this clash with him over the issue of his son's traffic summons I considered Beekay to be a highly valued friend. He regularly sat in the Goomalling Court of Petty Sessions with other Justices of the Peace or the Magistrate. And had often praised me after Court on the fair manner in which I gave evidence and presented my case. As the proprietor of the close-by general agency and hardware store his accessibility made it convenient to consider Beekay first, whenever a Justice of the Peace was required. So we had a lot to do with him on an official basis.

On a personal level he helped me a lot. With a young family my finances were always stretched to meet hire-purchase payments and general living expenses. It was hard to find the extra cash needed to buy some desired (but non-essential) items, such as birthday or christmas presents for the kids. So when Beekay offered me the opportunity of purchasing such "special" items through his store on an informal time-payment basis, I naively accepted. And over a period of twelve months or so I bought several items in this manner. Of course I made only limited use of the facility and cleared the debt as soon as I could.

Around this period many teenage youths in the

district owned or had access to modern fast cars and, as many teenagers unfortunately do, were prone to drive too fast or "sky-lark" recklessly to impress their mates. Some lost their lives because of this. In the 1950's and for several decades later country Traffic law enforcement was the responsibility of the relevant Local Government Authority – known then as "Roads Boards" – in this instance the Goomalling Roads Board. Some of the larger Local Government Authorities employed a full time Traffic Inspector or combined with other Roads Boards to do so. Smaller Roads Boards, such as Goomalling, simply nominated their Secretary as their "Traffic Inspector".

Apart from those localities where a full-time Traffic Inspector operated, Traffic Law enforcement in country areas was minimal or non-existent. Generally the police role mainly consisted of assisting the Roads Board Traffic Inspector (the Secretary) when asked to do so. However in practice we took direct action against unlicensed drivers and often stepped in to prosecute persons who drove dangerously within the townsite. Such was the system that operated at Goomalling. The "young bloods" were given a warning (where appropriate) about their driving and if they continued we summoned them. The Local Authority was happy with the arrangement and a degree of traffic control existed. Ironically Beekay was usually one of the Justices who dealt with the traffic charges Police brought before the Court, and, after dealing with matter, he often appropriately lectured the (usually) young offender for his stupidity.

Now young Beekay was no better or worse than any of the other teenage drivers about town and I had warned him at least once to "take it easy", but it made little difference to his driving. The crunch came during a particularly busy period for me – Tubby again being off sick – when I returned home at about four o-clock one Saturday afternoon to find my wife (who was expecting the birth of our third child) quite distraught. She explained that a short time before, attracted by the noise of a high

Rodney and Colleen on the bike.

revving car engine, she looked through the kitchen window to see a light colour Holden sedan sliding almost broadside around the street corner near our home. Our two little children were on the outside of our front yard fence and she screamed in horror as the vehicle slewed directly towards them.

Our home was at the junction of two unsealed town streets. The street which the house faced was the stem of the T and had a concave shaped surface with raised earth shoulders at either side. As the sliding car struck the raised earth shoulder of the road, less than 10 feet (approx 3 m) from our kids, the impact caused it to straighten up and it accelerated away down the road. My wife recognised the car as young Beekay's. He was driving and had two or three others in the car with him. She pointed out the deep gouge marks on the surface of the earth road, where the car had slewed around the corner and struck the shoulder in front of our fence. Using flour I carefully marked out these tracks so a detailed plan could later be prepared for presentation in Court.

I found young Beekay a short time later in the main street with his friends. He agreed he was driving and that the car did slide as he took the corner near my home. We returned to the scene together where he confirmed the marks on the road were made by his car. His explanation was that he had moved out a little wide on the corner because of a small tree branch (now no-where to be seen) lying on the road. He denied he was travelling too fast and claimed the vehicle was always under his control – even when skidding towards my children whom he saw near the fence. He was rather casual about the whole thing and was quite prepared to give me a written statement. After taking his statement I told him I didn't accept his explanation and intended to charge him on summons with Reckless Driving to appear before the Magistrate on his next visit.

Although Tubby was not officially on duty I let him know what had happened and the action I intended to take, as I anticipated a hostile reaction from Beekay. So I was a little apprehensive as I took the prepared Traffic Summons to Beekay's home later that afternoon. It was my intention to serve the summons on Beekay junior in his father's presence – perhaps getting him to concede the basic facts again in front of his father. But he was not at home and Beekay wanted to know what it was all about. When I explained what had taken place to cause me to take the action I had, Beekay surprised me when he adopted a responsible attitude. As he calmly accepted the summons for his son, he said, "I'm actually glad this has happened. The silly young fool needs to be pulled into line before he harms himself or somebody else."

Although I was nonplussed by Beekay's reaction (because of his previous outburst) I tried to gain further support as I said, "I'm glad we agree Beekay. If you can spare a few minutes now why not come with me and I'll show you the broad-side marks he left on the road as he came around the corner?"

Beekay agreed and followed me home in his car. We looked closely at the tyre tracks marked out on the road and I explained what my wife told me had happened. Then we walked back to his car parked in front of our home as my wife came out to join us. I was astonished at Beekay's sincerity as he apologized to my wife for his son's behaviour and then went on into a little speech about his intentions.

I clearly recall his words. Beekay said, "Mrs Primrose, I want to apologize for the way my son frightened you this afternoon. I can understand how you felt and I want you to know that, regardless of what penalty the Magistrate may impose, he won't be driving his car as from today". My wife thanked Beekay and, as he drove away, turning to me she said, "Well what a nice man! I really don't know why you were so worried that he'd be hostile about you summoning his son."

"I don't know," I said, "something isn't right. That didn't sound like Beekay talking there. I'd be surprised if it's over yet."

And it certainly wasn't. Within a half hour he was back. This time accompanied by Beekay junior. He parked the car in front of our home and walked back to the corner with his son. They only spent a couple of minutes there before coming into our yard. I walked out to meet them as they came up the front path. Beekay had the summons in his hand and I could tell by the enraged look on his face that he was furious. He angrily thrust the summons at me and said, "You will withdraw this! It's all a put up job! I've discussed it with my son and he's given me a perfectly reasonable explanation for what happened. There was no danger to anyone. You'll take it back!"

"I have no intention of taking it back Beekay." I replied.

"If you don't it will be thrown out of Court. I'll see to that! There's no evidence." He continued.

"Well I believe there is" I said. Then I continued (probably fuelling his anger) "I am fully prepared for a defended charge as unfortunately this was the attitude I expected you to take. So we'll leave it for the Magistrate to decide."

"I'm tellin' you if you don't withdraw this bloody summons, by the time I'm finished with you they'll run you out of town on a greasy pole!" Beekay snarled, almost white with rage.

"We'll see." I said as I turned away – there was little point in arguing any further. Beekay and his son then returned to the car and drove away.

The first indication of the debacle I was about to become involved in occurred the following Monday. I received a telephone call from my Regional Superintendent who told me he was aware I had taken action by summons against young Beekay for Reckless Driving. He instructed me to have the charge adjourned "sine die" (that is, adjourned indefinitely)

A few days later the Superintendent arrived at Goomalling and questioned me closely on a number of "technical" details connected with the charge. For example – why didn't I record the complaint from my wife in the station occurrence Book? Why didn't I record the inquiries I made; the interview with Beekay's son; the service of the summons and so on? I was amazed he should question me on such trivial matters. The Superintendent was well aware of the operational difficulties I had due to the extra work-load caused by Tubby's absence on sick leave. In practice, particularly when you're "under the hammer", most of the minor details he referred to are never recorded.

Then he dropped a bombshell. He showed me a written statement he had taken from Beekay. It was a totally malicious document. Among his many complaints about me he stated I was an officious policeman who was always harassing local teenagers over minor traffic matters. He claimed that, because of his position as a Justice of the Peace, he had been compelled to speak to me about my unacceptable behaviour on a number of occasions. That I resented this and set out to "get" his son. The document went on and on slamming me in every way; claiming that in regard to the summons charge I had bullied and threatened his son with physical assault unless he signed the "false" statement I had written out. He even claimed he had spoken to my wife and she was surprised that I had summoned his son on such a trivial matter. Throughout the whole statement I was portrayed as a "foul mouthed" Police bully. I was dumbfounded by the viciousness of his attack.

The Superintendent gave me just one hour to submit a detailed report in answer to Beekay's many complaints. Although the time factor placed me under great pressure – because of the status of the complainant and the very serious nature of his complaint – I did the best I could and completed the report by this deadline. Then, as the weeks passed without any word from the Superintendent on the outcome of his investigation, the pressure on me became even greater. The town was abuzz with discussion about the likely result of Beekay's complaint. It seemed there was no limit to his vindictiveness for he tried to discredit me at every opportunity, and many believed him. It was a terrible time.

On the other hand it heartened me that many genuine townspeople contacted me to express their support and to ask my version of the incident. I was particularly pleased when the local Catholic Priest telephoned me and asked me around for coffee, so we might discuss the matter. I wasn't one of his flock, yet he was concerned about what appeared to be happening or what might happen to me if even half the rumours were true. After I explained the situation to him, Father said, "You may not know it Bob but I'm a personal friend of your Commissioner and I would be happy to speak with him on your behalf."

I was impressed but declined. I said, "Thank you Father but I don't think that should be necessary at present as I haven't done anything wrong, and I hope that this will be shown to be so." Then I added (with a laugh) "But if you don't mind I'll take a rain-check on your offer – just in case someone "up top" believes Beekay's lies and I am to be charged or disciplined."

Finally it was about two months before I was advised my Regional Officer had found nothing to support any of Beekay's allegations against me, whereas he found ample evidence to confirm my version of the events leading to Beekay's son being charged with the Traffic offence.

Likewise the Superintendent confirmed that, prior to the issue of the traffic summons against Beekay's son, Beekay and I had been good friends. Nevertheless, the Superintendent reported, I had technically erred by becoming involved in Traffic Law enforcement when it was not "Policy" to do so – particularly when my wife was the complainant. However, he stated, the traffic charge itself was correctly laid and there was ample evidence to obtain a conviction. Therefore the action commenced by police was being withdrawn and a Traffic prosecution brief, prepared by the Officer in charge of the Police Traffic Branch, was being forwarded to the Local Authority (Goomalling Road Board) with a recommendation that they prosecute young Beekay for Reckless Driving. It was a qualified "slap on the wrist" for me when the charge was withdrawn but there was nothing I could do about it.

However the battle was still far from over, as Beekay apparently considered that the Roads Board was an easier target for him to intimidate. He spread the word (through contacts on the Council) that he had "inside" information that the Police charge was withdrawn because it would fail and be deemed a "malicious prosecution". If the Local Authority took up the prosecution it would also fail and considerable damages would then be awarded against the Council instead of the Police. Such was Beekay's influence that he nearly succeeded. Many on the Council believed him and the debate, on whether to proceed or not, raged for months without a final decision being made.

Under what is known as "The statute of limitation" a

complaint under the Traffic Act must be made within six months of the date of the offence. At the time the original Police charge was withdrawn, over two months had already elapsed, therefore the Roads Board had less than four months in which to proceed. But the Police Department too kept up the pressure. As each month passed, the Secretary of the Goomalling Roads Board received correspondence from the Police Department asking if the Council had yet made their decision. Finally, such was their confusion, the Roads Board asked one of Perth's leading Barristers, Mr Ken Hatfield QC, for an opinion on the probability of a successful prosecution. As I was later told, he virtually said "it's a piece of cake" – so they engaged him to prosecute the case. Determined to the last, Beekay engaged an equally eminent Barrister, Mr George Gwynne QC, to defend his son.

It was ludicrous. The lesser town hall was used as the Court of Petty Sessions with a relatively straight-forward Traffic charge (Reckless Driving) to be decided by the Magistrate, and two of the state's leading Barristers to argue the merits of the case. The evidence for the prosecution was effective and uncomplicated. The final crunch came when defence counsel, unable to shake my evidence, attempted to attack my credibility by trying to introduce much of the original rubbish Beekay had alleged about me.

When I refused to agree with any of the matters he put to me, the Barrister finally said, "Isn't it a fact that there has been bad blood between you and the defendant's father for some time?" (ah hah! – a trick question this one!)

"On the contrary ..." I began.

"Answer the question Constable – Yes or No if you please" he cut me off – attempting to force an answer he could attack. I ignored the tactic and turning to the Magistrate I asked his permission to answer the question fully in my own way. He agreed.

I briefly explained the good relationship I had with

Beekay until I charged his son – I concluded by saying "…and in fact, at the time, I was in his debt for over fifty pounds ($100) – the balance I owed on a typewriter he purchased for me through his business – a debt I cleared as soon as this matter arose."

Beekay had obviously not told the Barrister the truth about our relationship for he seemed quite surprised by my answer. Seeking leave of the Court, Mr Gwynne quickly conferred with Beekay – who must have confirmed what I said was correct – then he advised the Magistrate he had no further questions to ask of me. So, with "personalities" out of the way, the hearing proceeded and Beekay junior was convicted on the charge of Reckless Driving.

After the Magistrate had imposed an appropriate fine and license suspension the subject of "Costs" was discussed. When any matter is dealt with by a Court the successful party is entitled to claim and be awarded "reasonable" costs – such as the legal fees paid to initiate the action and the costs of engaging legal counsel. With a wry smile, the Magistrate addressed the two Barristers standing before him, and said "I must say gentlemen, it is not often that a Country Court dealing with a relatively minor traffic charge is blessed with the presence of two such eminent Counsel. And while I appreciate that both parties may have incurred substantial costs by engaging you, the complexity of the matter does not justify the award of the costs your presence would otherwise demand, when the matter might well have been adequately handled by less learned Counsel at reasonable cost. Solicitors fees of two hundred pounds ($400) would seem to me, to be "reasonable costs" in this instance and I so award such costs against the defendant in addition to the normal Court costs."

And so it was over. Beekay's intimidation of the Goomalling Roads Board Committee – causing their indecision and referral of the matter for Queen's Counsel decision – cost them at least one thousand pounds ($2000) for Court attendance alone. Likewise it was rumoured that the fee for the Barrister defending Beekay's son was also $2000. But for me it was like finally having a great weight lifted from my shoulders. Justice had been done, and was also seen to be done. Whenever I now hear the quote "there is no such thing as a free lunch" I always think of "my friend" Beekay.

*   *   *   *   *

Tubby Eaton's replacement as the O.I.C of Goomalling Police station, Constable Robert C. Gilchrist, was also a very capable and experienced country policeman. Bob was different in many ways to Tubby. And at first there was some friction – as you might expect at the beginning of any new relationship – but we soon sorted things out, became friends and worked well together in an effective partnership.

As I have mentioned before, police wages were not all that good and living costs were high. With our young family growing, financial juggling became an art form. Opportunities to earn extra money were rare but my new boss Bob Gilchrist, who was sensitive to my needs, allowed me to take up quite a bit of seasonal farm-labouring work after-hours or on my days off – covering for me if I worked a late ploughing shift at seeding time. And so we survived, met our commitments and slowly started to get ahead. Thinking back now on my time with Tubby Eaton, I believe he had the ability and potential to have progressed to a senior level within the Police Force, but that was not his ambition. All he really wanted was to remain at middle management level in a Country posting. After only seven months in the metropolitan area Tubby moved to the country again – a Sergeant position at Kalgoorlie. Then in January 1964 he was appointed as the Sergeant in charge of Boulder Police station, a position he held until his tragic death on April 1, 1970 following a freak accident at the Boulder Speedway – an out of control hot-rod vehicle struck the spectator enclosure safety fence; a wheel flew off, cleared the fence and struck Tubby, shattering his thigh-bone. Complications arising from this injury later caused his death in Royal Perth Hospital. At age fifty one, Tubby's passing was a sad loss not only for his family and many friends, but also for the community whom he served.

"Tubby" Eaton – taken a few years before his death when he was Sergeant in Charge of Boulder Police Station.

CHAPTER TEN.

Armed and Dangerous

Quite some time after severing my connection with the St John Ambulance Committee, I eventually agreed to assist another local community organization by taking up the position of Secretary – the vacancy having been created by the imminent transfer of the current holder; Alan Wilkerson, Manager of the Goomalling Branch of the National Bank.

At about eight one evening I was at the Police station with Alan discussing the duties of the position I was to take over from him, when the telephone rang. It was the lady who operated the Roadhouse/Service station on the main road.

Earlier that day I had received an all stations "Urgent, Look-out To Be Kept For Escapees" (Urgent L.T.B.K.F Escapees) police message, advising that three seventeen year old youths had broken out of a Prisons Dept institution the night before. The escapees were thought to be armed and dangerous. They were the prime suspects for an overnight raid on a firearms store in Midland and the theft of a cream colour Ford utility (in which they were thought to be travelling). The message included detailed descriptions of the escapees – each of whom had previous criminal convictions – and cautioned that extreme care should be exercised in approaching them.

They were believed to possess a number of weapons, including shotguns, high-powered rifles and ammunition, and a range of camping gear and clothing stolen from the gun store.

As with all police L.T.B.K.F. messages, all service stations and other likely points of contact within our District had been asked to assist and provided with basic details of the escapees and the utility. Similarly the message had also been passed on to police at other stations adjoining our District. No indication had been given of the route the escapees were expected to take. There was nothing unusual about this particular message. Messages such as this are relatively common.

The Roadhouse proprietor said (in relation to the L.T.B.K.F message) "You know that message you gave us today about the young men with the stolen utility? Well a little while ago a nice young chap came in and wanted a jerrycan filled with petrol. I thought it seemed a bit strange, because he came from a utility parked down the road a bit. I couldn't get the number but I really don't think it's the utility you're looking for as he was such a polite young man and cleanly dressed, but I thought I should let you know anyway just in case."

I thanked her; told her I'd check it out and hung up the phone. Moving quickly to the firearm storage cabinet, I took out a .38 revolver and loaded it with ammunition as I turned to Alan Wilkerson and said, "Alan, what about coming with me while I check out a stolen car report?" (my boss Constable Bob Gilchrist was away on holiday at the time)

"Hell!" he exclaimed, "What's the gun for?"

I briefly explained the L.T.B.K.F message and the telephone call from the Roadhouse, and added "I don't really think it will be them, and even if it was they're probably miles away by now, but I'm taking a revolver with me as a precaution anyway."

He agreed and we were off in my car to the Roadhouse, but, as I had predicted, there was no sign of the utility. I checked around the town streets and main road exits radiating north south and to the west but again found nothing. Then doubling back through the Reserve on the north side of the Railway station, I stopped to allow a north-bound vehicle to pass in front of me as I waited to rejoin the main road.

By this time I'd decided I had done enough; any further searching was pointless; even if it had been the escapees in the utility reportedly seen near the Roadhouse they were well gone by now. It was over. Time for Alan and me to return to the station and resume our discussion about the secretarial postion.

Then with a gut-wrenching jolt my senses sprang alert. In the headlights of my car I saw that the passing vehicle fitted the description of the stolen utility referred to in the L.T.B.K.F. message. It was a cream coloured Ford utility with three men in the cab. The vehicle was obviously carrying a heavy load (later confirmed to be the stolen arms and camping gear) as it was well down at the rear.

I turned my vehicle to follow and could see by the license number that it really was the stolen utility. My heartbeat seemed to leap into overdrive and my mind, dismayed at the enormity of the situation, struggled to keep pace. The juvenile criminals I was about to deal with had a history of violence. In escaping from prison they had immediately armed and equipped themselves in a manner that at least suggested they were prepared for a "shoot out" to avoid recapture. Whereas I was armed with only a .38 calibre 6 shot revolver and had the backing of one un-armed civilian of unknown capability. The odds were against me but there was no time or source for me to obtain any other back-up. In a head-on confrontation I faced a seemingly hopeless situation. The only factor in my favour was the element of surprise. I desperately tried to focus my mind on just how to make the most of this small advantage in the few seconds that elapsed before the action started.

Then it was on! This was it! My one chance! Both

vehicles had been travelling fairly slowly, about fifty metres apart, before the stolen utility suddenly stopped at a T junction about one hundred and fifty metres further up the rise while the occupants examined a road direction sign with a spotlight. They probably didn't know it was the police in the vehicle following them. There was no way to tell. If they were expecting me I was a "gonner". As they stopped the utility I braked to a stop less than a car's length behind, and leapt out with the loaded revolver in my hand.

In the seconds that elapsed as I ran forward to the driver's side window, I firmly believed there was a good chance I would be shot, possibly killed. There was no time for fear: if anyone started shooting I was not going to be far behind. If I was to be shot I would be taking someone with me. The thought caused my adrenalin to peak as I covered the last metre or so cocking the revolver as I ran – pulling back the hammer and reducing the trigger firing mechanism to a single action pull (in effect from a 12lb pressure pull to a 3lb trigger pressure). With the wisdom of hindsight, as I am sure the "arm-chair" critics would agree, this was an extremely dangerous and foolish thing to do. But in a situation like this when you believe your life is on the line it is very hard to think clearly, where even a moments hesitation could mean the difference between your life or death. I was as tight as a drum with tension as I thrust the revolver through the open window against the driver's head identifying myself and barking instructions. I could see by the light of the spotlight they were using, there was a shotgun (later found to be loaded) lying across their laps. I ordered them to place their hands behind their heads and threatened to shoot if they attempted to bring up the shotgun.

The vehicle was "hot wired" so I told the driver to carefully apply the hand brake and foot brake, and to stall the engine in gear. I kept the revolver pressed against his head and continued my warnings as he did so. Then I had him pass out the shotgun butt first from the cab. I placed the gun on the road under the vehicle before ordering the three of them out to stand against the side of the utility with their hands still behind their heads.

The driver, who had been scared witless by my revolver pressed to his head, quickly complied but his two companions were slow to do so and became insolent and threatening. Realizing I was on my own they were clearly sizing me up and assessing their chances of escape. The three of them were big young men, only just under the age of eighteen and each was taller and heavier than either Alan or me, so in a physical contest the 3/2 odds would have definitely been in their favour. But I was armed and determined and I never let them forget that for a moment as I threatened and pushed them (prodding them with the revolver) until I had them all standing facing away from me against the side of the utility with their hands clasped behind their heads.

By now my civilian helper, Alan, had joined me. God knows what he was thinking. How could he, within the space of a few minutes, have become involved in such a dangerous and volatile situation. At my request Alan got my (one pair) handcuffs from the glove-box of the car. As he returned with them, and I thought of having him take the revolver while I searched and handcuffed my prisoners, the full gravity of the extremely dangerous situation I had created (by cocking the action of the revolver) struck home. I had been prodding these young men with a loaded weapon, set to fire with almost "hair trigger" pressure.

I started to shake as I turned the gun away from them attempting to uncock the action. But I was shaking so much my fingers slipped from the hammer as I tried to release it from the ready fire position and the revolver discharged harmlessly onto the road. You can imagine the sobering effect that the noise of the shot discharging and the flash of flame had on everyone, me included. But for the benefit of my prisoners I made out I had intended to fire a shot as, steeling myself, I said "That's just to let you know I'm not playing games."

After the revolver accidentally went off, the casual attitude of the escapees changed and they meekly complied. Handing the now safe weapon to Alan, I searched them and handcuffed two of them together and placed the three of them in my car under Alan's guard, whilst I retrieved the shotgun from under the utility and placed it (with other prime weapons taken from the back of the utility) in the boot of my car. As I drove back to the Police station with our prisoners (Alan guarding them with the revolver) I tried to appear calm but inwardly I was still very nervous, feeling a bit like an over-tightened spring and I knew that Alan must have been feeling the same. The escapees seemed to sense this and were starting to "thaw out", insolently referring to me as "the copper" and bragging about what they would have done if I hadn't "got the drop on them". They had dressed themselves in some of the new clothing stolen from the store in Midland. Each wore heavy fur-lined boots, leather jackets and denim shirts and trousers. As they swaggered into my office one of them, in a intimidatory move, put his boot through the fly wire door ripping away the netting. Oh yes they thought it was a great joke alright! It was time for me to re-establish who was in control.

I ordered the two handcuffed together to sit on the office floor and, leaving Alan to guard them, I took the other escapee into the cell block. He protested when I made him remove all the stolen clothing he had on, leaving him with only his underclothes locked in a cell alone. Then I repeated the process with the other two, one at a time. And as their "flash gear" came off, and they were segregated from each other, no longer able to feed on each other's bravado with only blankets for cover and company, their theatrical toughness melted to pitiful embarrassment. No longer armed and dangerous they were just pathetic young men. I even felt sorry for them. They seemed to have no idea how their stupid criminal behaviour could so easily have ended in tragedy, and their lives, my life or all our lives could have been ruined forever.

* * * * *

My posting to the second man position at Goomalling at such an early stage in my service career, was a real bonus. But on the other hand it was frustrating not to be able to progress any further for such a long time. After three or four years at Goomalling and relief work at various other small stations in the Eastern Wheatbelt region I gained a good knowledge of country police station management, but constantly failed to win selection for any of the advertised vacancies I sought – simply because of seniority. Never-the-less I persevered.

Finally it was almost exactly six years before I succeeded, and even then it was not the position of my choice. The policy was that if several members applied for an advertised position, the most senior applicant was chosen – unless a more junior applicant was considered far more capable or deserving (rarely did this occur). If the successful applicant already held a lower level O.I.C position elsewhere the position he was vacating would be offered to the next-in-line. This was known as a "consequential" transfer.

I had applied for the position of O.I.C. at Wongan Hills – a two man Police station. Constable Tom Clews (who was much my senior) was selected and I was offered the one man position he was vacating at Gwalia – a small ramshackle goldmining town near Leonora, about 240 kms North of Kalgoorlie and 800 kms from Perth. It wasn't the best place to take a young family, but the policy was that if you accepted such a posting, and performed well, you enhanced your chances of getting a much better position later on.

I accepted the transfer to Gwalia as Officer in Charge and so opened a new chapter in my life as a policeman.

123

CHAPTER ELEVEN

Suburban Beat – Innaloo

After a fairly intense three years as the sole policeman at Gwalia – described in my first book "Mister Bob" – family health reasons caused me to apply to return to the Perth Metropolitan area. My return to city policing after nine years at country stations was a disappointing change I hadn't planned.

The Police District of Innaloo, located in the north western metropolitan area of Perth, was created by the take-over of some areas previously under the control of Scarborough and Mount Hawthorn Police. It included areas of sprawling market gardens, housing development, quality freehold properties and Government rental homes, with a working-class to upper middle-class population. The station had an allocated staff of two, and my boss, Sergeant Charlie Watts the officer in charge, had taken up his appointment only a week or two before I arrived from Gwalia. So it was a new start for both of us.

Charlie was a good bloke to work with and we got on well. I was used to working alone in the community and made good use of my country police experience to help establish the framework of a good Police/Community relationship. I found it easy to slip into the "village constable" role, and as I motored about on inquiries I regularly called on and got to know many business proprietors, Justices of the Peace and quite a few long term residents of the District who were all a great help as we sought to become familiar with our area.

Particularly in the early period, the sheer volume of mundane paperwork we handled rarely left much time for anything else. In the early 60's practically all the paperwork which is now dealt with by post, was handled by police at suburban stations or special sections in the city. So initially most of my time was spent trying to get on top of a never-ending mountain of simple traffic related files and summonses. There was little challenge in the work and after the varied life of a country policeman I found it rather dull. However I applied the philosophy

Rodney, Gregory and Colleen.

125

that you can make any job as interesting or as boring as you want to, and got on with the job.

One of my early difficulties was my lack of experience with a motorcycle/sidecar combination. The Police Department had provided the station with a new BSA "Goldflash" 650cc motorcycle with an old sidecar attached, as our means of transport. It was a powerful machine – really a bit too powerful for the old sidecar and it was a damn awkward machine to steer (seemed to have a mind of it's own), particularly on a left turn or when there was no passenger in the sidecar. I hadn't ridden a motorcycle since learning to ride while in the Police school ten years before, and I had no experience at all with the motorcycle/sidecar combination. So during the first week or two at Innaloo it was more or less a learning/re-learning experience for me. I wasn't game to ride it while in full uniform as I seemed to be making such a spectacle of myself. But I soon got the hang of it and became a competent rider.

Initially I apparently upset a few people when I did as I was required to do and properly checked their entitlement to a Market Gardener's, (vehicle) Concession License. Genuine market gardeners as "Primary producers", are entitled to a reduction of the license fee on a vehicle they use solely for "farming" purposes. In those days when a market gardener first made application, their bona fides would be checked by police before the concession was granted. Subsequent renewals were supposed to be dealt with in the same manner. However it seemed that in the past this was rarely done, particularly in the case of renewals. Often the constable concerned simply assumed the market gardener's circumstances were correct or unchanged and recommended renewal of the concession without making a proper check. But when Innaloo police became responsible for verifying applications, I always inspected the property and spoke with the license holder before making a recommendation. Although I found the majority to be genuine market gardeners, I found quite a few applicants who were attempting to rort the system. In one instance the area supposed to be a market garden had been sub-divided years before and built on as a housing development. The address on the renewal application was correct, but the only produce grown by the applicant was in his small back-yard vegetable patch. He was a wealthy man no longer working as a market gardener, yet he claimed he was entitled to retain his concession as he took an occasional box of produce to market. There were others who had retired on the "age pension" and still wanted to claim they were genuine market gardeners, even though another family member now operated the market garden as their own business.

Probably the most blatant was a bloke who operated a motorcycle sales and repair business in the city. His utility, licensed under concession ostensibly for his use as a primary producer, was plastered with signs advertising his motorcycle business and was obviously an integral part of that business. He was surprised and annoyed when I insisted on attending the Balcatta property with him to check on his alleged cattle farming activities, and to see some of the cattle he claimed were there. After we spent about a half hour wandering through some of his wooded and uncleared land, while he made the pretence of trying to find them, surprise surprise; he "suddenly remembered" having moved all his cattle to a property he owned at Harvey. He became angry when I told him I would not recommend renewal of his vehicle license concession for the Balcatta property. I also found it interesting when word was passed to me, on more than one occasion, that "so-an-so" (about to be reviewed as a Concession license holder) was related to certain members of the Police Force in the Traffic Branch. I wondered what difference they thought that should have made.

These days Commonwealth legislation – the Service and Execution of Process Act 1992 – provides the authority for police throughout Australia to serve and execute processes issued in other states. Prior to late 1965 there was no such reciprocal arrangement. For although the Commonwealth legislation then in force provided for the service of inter-state summonses, payment of the fines and costs (or other penalty) then imposed by the Court could not be enforced. It was an almost laughable situation. Few if any of the inter-state hauliers would pay fines imposed on them by courts in the other states for offences such as speeding or over-loading. Warrants would then be issued and sent to Police in this state for execution, either by payment in full or the arrest of the truckie to serve a term of imprisonment in default. It was a game: On receipt of the Warrant I'd locate the truckie at home between trips or leave a message for him to call at the station. I then had to ask if he would pay the amount on the warrant. None ever did; they preferred to take the chance of being stopped by police as they travelled through the state concerned. I suppose you couldn't blame the truckies for putting off payment until the very last. But the amount of their outstanding inter-state fines grew and some of them had great difficulty in meeting payment when caught on the road. There were rumours about truckies arrested "on road" inter-state, whose loads were sometimes left unattended for days while they tried to raise the cash or arranged for another haulier.

Finally late in 1965 the Commonwealth law changed; we were then not only required to serve the inter-state processes but also to execute the warrants if the fines were not paid. A number of inter-state truckies lived in the Innaloo area, and I knew them all well, most of them had outstanding inter-state fines. The Warrants we had previously sent back were returned for execution, it was my job to sort it all out. As expected a few grumbled about now having to pay (the alternative of serving time in gaol being unattractive) but when I explained the law change most of them accepted the unavoidable and paid up. Sometimes, when I knew the particular truckie was hard-pushed for cash, we allowed him sufficient time to raise the amount required. It was mostly achieved in an air of co-operation, but as is often the case there always seems to be some ornery "B" who is unwilling to accept the inevitable. This was the case with Sam Vitza (not his real name).

I had only one inter-state warrant for Sam. It seems he'd been caught on the road in Queensland a few weeks before and forced to clear up most of his outstanding fines. Sam was away a lot and I called often at his home over several weeks but missed him each time. Although I left verbal and written messages with Sam's wife, explaining the situation and asking Sam to contact the station, he ignored my requests. He knew why I wanted to see him (my messages had been quite clear) but after a night or two at home he'd be off again without bothering to phone or call in. I had to take a firmer stand. I had the warrant with me one Friday evening when I saw Sam's prime mover truck parked outside his home. It was about 8pm. I parked the motorcycle/sidecar outside and rang the doorbell. An un-smiling Sam appeared at the door, breathing beery breath on me as he asked, "What do you want?"

"You know what I want Sam." I said, "You got my messages about the inter-state warrants didn't you?"

"So what! You know I don't pay on inter-state warrants unless they catch me on the road over east."

"As I explained in the note I left you Sam, it's all been changed and we now have to execute inter-state warrants."

"I'm not payin'. My solicitor has told me I don't have to pay."

"Well he's wrong. The law has been changed and now you do have to pay."

"You can get stuffed! I'm not payin'."

"Well if you won't pay I'll have to execute the warrant and arrest you."

"What! you! You arrest ME?" he exclaimed belligerently, "The last time the coppers arrested me in Queensland it took six of them, and they wouldn't have succeeded then if they hadn't put a 303 rifle to my head."

Now Sam was a strongly built man over 6 feet (183 cm) tall, but I wasn't going to be intimidated that easily. Policemen often achieve their objectives by bluff, and this was the tactic I first chose as I quickly replied, "Oh we can all be tough can't we. If I have to arrest you I will." Then (rather foolishly) I added, "I used to eat two or three blokes your size before breakfast in the Goldfields."

"Oh yeah?" He rubbed his hands together and stepped forward on the verandah, "Out on the lawn then, and let's see how good you are."

Whoops! The alarm bells rang in my head as I quickly assessed the situation and reformed my strategy. I was on my own. There was no chance of anyone helping, or me calling for assistance. I was on the verge of a fight with a bloke who was bigger and physically stronger than me and even if I was able to over-power him I had only the motorcycle combination for transport. There had to be a better way and there was. The common sense approach I should have used in the first place.

"Whoa!" I said, "Stop right there. This is ridiculous. It isn't between you and me. It's between you and the law. If we step out on the lawn now to try and settle this, you might belt the hell out of me but then you might not. Either way you're going to lose and get yourself into very serious trouble."

I went on to suggest that the intelligent thing for him to do would be to give me his cheque to cover the amount, allowing me to satisfy the warrant and leave. This would give him ample time to query his solicitor's advice, and he could (if he chose) then cancel the cheque. But I warned again that the solicitor was wrong and that if the cheque was not honoured, I would return later with a back-up and he would be arrested to serve the default. A stony silence prevailed as Sam glared at me for several seconds. Then I breathed a sigh of relief as he re-entered his home to get his cheque book, wrote a cheque for the amount required on the warrant and handed it to me without speaking. I thanked him and left. A satisfactory conclusion had been negotiated allowing both of us to "save face". Oh yes, when presented Sam's cheque was honoured.

Although my "bluff" tactic didn't work too well with Sam (I probably only got out of that tricky situation by the skin of my teeth) there are many occasions when a policeman finds the odds stacked against him, and bluff seems the only way out. You just have to take the chance and hope it works. One typical situation, where (luckily) it did work, was a confrontation I had one night with Tony Ablich (not his real name) a heavily built, slightly "gone to seed", psycho maintenance defaulter.

For many years when a person failed to make maintenance payments ordered by the Court (eg. to assist in the support of a child or spouse), the Court eventually issued a warrant for the arrest of the defaulter to serve a gaol term in lieu of payment. Much police time (and resources) was wasted trying to trace these maintenance defaulters, and although a lot of them paid up when located many opted to serve the time rather than pay. It was an impractical expensive system which has since been abolished.

Tony, who was of Yugoslavian birth, apparently owned his home at Balcatta and other investment property. He was separated from his wife and children and she obtained a maintenance order against him for their support. Tony wouldn't pay, so from time to time a Maintenance Default Warrant arrived at Innaloo for his arrest. I never had any real trouble with him and while he grumbled about having to pay the arrears he always did. Although he wasn't certifiable, Tony was a real "strange one" and often made incomprehensible remarks; the sort of a bloke you always had to handle with kid gloves.

Then a change occurred. Tony no longer co-operated and became aggressive towards anyone and everyone, family included. Tony's full name was Ante Luka Ablich, the name shown on Court documents but he insisted he was not that person; he was another man named Tony Ablich, the name he was commonly known by. About this time he also started to drink heavily and frequent night-clubs. The inevitable happened. He got into a fight one night at a night-club and the police were called. Now although Tony's 18 stone (115 kg) frame was a bit flabby he was still a big powerful man, and with his "strange" mental state further affected by liquor, he was a real handful for the four policemen who attended.

Then two or three weeks after this incident we received another Maintenance Default Warrant for him. I checked with Tony's elderly relatives and learnt he was aware the warrant had been issued and was moving about, staying a night or two here or there to avoid police. He ignored my messages to make contact and his relatives warned me to expect trouble if I attempted to arrest him on the warrant. Because of this warning and the difficulty police had with Tony the last time he was arrested, I had no intention of tackling him on my own. I planned to ask Central Police for a security van crew as back-up. The relatives co-operated (they too were frightened of Tony in his volatile state) and they agreed to let me know when he was next expected at his parents home for a meal.

The call came about 6.30pm a few nights later; Tony was expected there at 7pm. I telephoned Central Police station, explained the situation to the Reserve Constable and asked that the van crew be sent out to pick me up at about 7.30pm, and go with me while I arrested Tony on the maintenance warrant.

"How do you know for sure that he'll be there?" asked the ornery Reserve Constable.

"Well I'm pretty sure. His parents expect him."

"Not good enough," he went on (giving me a little lecture about the lack of resources), "You go and check, and if he's there I'll send out the Van."

In hindsight, what a ridiculous suggestion, and how foolish of me to have agreed. I was alone, had only a motorcycle combination for transport, no means of communication, and here I was going off in the dark to check on a man with a history of mental instability and recent violence. Tony's parents' home was half-way down a slight incline on North Beach Road Balcatta. I switched off the motorcycle's engine, turned off the lights and coasted down-hill to stop about 50 metres past their house. I was quietly making my way back to the house in the hope of attracting someone inside without alerting Tony (if he was there) when he suddenly walked from the house and came to meet me in the front yard.

"You lookin' for me?" he asked aggressively.

"Yes Tony, I am," I replied, taking the Maintenance Default Warrant from my tunic pocket, "I've come about this maintenance warrant."

"That's not for me." he said, "What's the name on the Warrant?"

"Ante Luka Ablich," I said, "And that's you."

"No it's not. My name's Tony. You even called me Tony just now. I'm not payin' someone else's maintenance."

"It is you Tony and if you won't pay I'll have to arrest you."

He looked at me in silence for a second or two, folded his arms across his chest and drawing himself up, he said, "Well you just try and arrest me then."

The adrenalin went spurt spurt as I folded the Warrant; placed it back in my tunic pocket; took a deep breath and, placing my hand on his left shoulder, I said "Okay you're under arrest."

To my great relief and surprise Tony just said, "Righto then," and quietly walked with me back to the motorcycle combination. I really expected him to explode at any minute and attack me, so I kept very alert as I helped him settle his bulky frame into the little sidecar. Then starting up the motorcycle I slowly rode back to the Innaloo Police station, Tony's excess weight flattening the sidecar springs and causing the combination to lean heavily.

Although he remained docile, I took no chances and handled Tony very carefully as I ushered him into the office, organised him a coffee and discreetly phoned

Central Police station for an urgent back-up. And to my relief the van crew, a Sergeant and two Constables, arrived shortly after. When the Sergeant saw Tony quietly sipping coffee in my office as he waited to be taken away in the security van, he pulled me aside and said, "Good grief! Do you know what you've got there? The man's a mad-man. I was in charge of the crew that arrested him a couple of weeks ago and what a time we had with him. How did you manage him on your own?"

"Just bluff Sergeant," I said, "Just bluff."

*　　*　　*　　*　　*

While I was stationed at Innaloo I spent a lot of time riding about on the motorcycle combination. Once I mastered it I found it a convenient means of moving about the District. It was easy to park or turn about in narrow streets and other confined spaces. Of course we had no such thing as a spot- light and I had to use a torch while steering with one hand to locate house numbers at night. It wasn't much fun in the rain but on summer evenings it was often quite pleasant. The coolness after the heat of the day; the heady fragrance of recently watered flower gardens filling the air. It was quite exhilarating and even made my mundane tasks seem worthwhile. I became very familiar with the area we policed and prided myself in eventually being able to go almost directly to any address and arrive there within a house number or two, which was a real bonus particularly in wet conditions at night. Fortunately I was never involved in an accident, although I do remember almost coming to grief (and making a fool of myself) one night. It was only luck (and a bit of riding skill) that saved me from going base-over-apex, but I'm sure those who witnessed the incident were not impressed.

There was an open-air picture theatre garden in Morris Place Innaloo, not far from the Police station, and on picture nights the area was usually congested with parked cars. It was also the popular gathering spot for

134

some of the unruly teenagers who lived in the area. Two or three of them had cars and liked to do the occasional "wheelie" to impress their mates, but most were pretty good kids who just had to be growled at occasionally to keep them in line.

I was about to leave the station one night when I heard the squeal of car tyres and, looking over, I saw a car come to a halt near a group of youths standing near other parked cars. It was interval time at the picture garden and people were streaming across the parking area towards the shops. I guessed (correctly) it was one of the local boys showing off for the picture crowd. I rode across on the motorcycle, stopped alongside the errant suspects, confirmed the culprit responsible for the wheel-spin, delivered a short sharp warning on what I'd do if he repeated the performance, then moved off, travelling east to circle the rows of parked cars before leaving Morris Place. The road surface at the south east corner of the parking area in Morris Place is slightly concave and I had to make a left turn at the end of the row of cars. But anxious to get away from the somewhat tense situation I had just created, I misjudged my speed. I wasn't even travelling fast, but the surface slope and the notorious left turn instability of a motorcycle combination combined to make the sidecar wheel rise clear of the road surface, and the motorcycle suddenly tipped sharply over. I was gone! About to crash! But because of my low speed I had a slim chance.

I kicked the road surface hard with my right foot at the same time wrenching the handlebars to force the machine back to a level plane and opened the throttle. The powerful motor responded with a roar and the rear wheel slipped and spun, burning rubber and screeching in protest as the motorcycle straightened up and sped forward scattering a group of amazed onlookers. I doubt whether anyone in the vicinity believed my wheelie was unintentional – least of all the group of young blokes I had just growled at.

As I rode rather shakily away, I could almost imagine one of them saying, "And that's the bastard that picked on US for showing off."

*   *   *   *   *

It was about 2pm and I had just returned from a visit to the City. As I parked the motorbike I could hear the phone ringing in the office. It was an operator at Police Communications.

"We've been trying to get you for at least a half hour. We've got a scrambled message about a woman having a snake bailed-up, or a snake having some woman bailed up in Paine Court Karrinyup."

"Great! (I hate dealing with snakes) Have you got a name and address?"

"No. That's all we've got. The caller hung up before we could get any details. You better get up there and check it out."

"Yeah, thanks a lot" (How I wished I'd stayed longer in the City).

Soon after – taking a garden rake and .38 calibre revolver as weapons of defence or attack – I left the station to check out the problem. I felt quite apprehensive about having to deal with a live snake, the only mitigating factor was that snakes don't usually hang around long after they've been disturbed. So there was a good chance it would be gone by the time I got there.

The Karrinyup locality was still being developed for housing at that time. A lot of building construction was taking place and roads were being put down and sealed. When I arrived in Paine Court it was a hive of activity. There was a road construction crew of about ten or so men with earth moving equipment and other gear in the street, and several teams of builders and bricklayers working on nearby houses. I relaxed a little. If there had been a snake surely one of these blokes would've despatched it by now.

136

At first the several workers I asked, knew nothing about a snake. Then one said, "Oh yes. It's in the lady's house over there," indicating the neat little Housing Commission home as he spoke.

"Oh damn!" I thought, "I've still got the problem to deal with."

The lady of the house answered my knock on her door. She told me that about an hour or so earlier she was sitting in her lounge watching television when, hearing a slight noise, she turned in her seat to see a large dark brown snake – which had probably entered through the open front door – slithering along the carpet. She screamed and (possibly becoming airborne) fled from the house to seek help from the nearby workers. A couple of them checked the house and found the snake in the bathroom (where it was now trapped) and closed the door. Someone phoned the police for her, as none of the workers wanted to tackle the snake in the confined space of the bathroom. (Never mind about policemen being scared of snakes, I thought.)

I carefully opened the closed door of the small bathroom, cold fingers of fear running up and down my spine as I scanned the floor for the snake. Suddenly there it was, a large brown dugite curled on the window-sill above the handbasin, forked tongue flicking and head darting about as it sensed my presence. Quickly closing the door I retreated to consider my options. The snake was trapped and anyone getting in its way would be attacked. Use of the revolver was out of the question and anyway a fast moving snake makes an almost impossible target. It had to be the garden rake, but I would need help.

The plan I formed was to pull the snake off the window-sill with the rake, pin it to the bathroom floor and have my assistant (yet to volunteer) kill it with a shovel. It seemed like a reasonable enough plan, but I had difficulty getting anyone to volunteer as they thought it too dangerous. Finally one of the road workers agreed to stand-by outside the house, until I had the snake pinned to the floor. He would then enter at my call and despatch the snake. It was the best I could do, no-one else wanted to be involved.

Putting my fear aside, I slowly opened the bathroom door again, the rake held ready. Then! Holy Hell! it all happened at once. The snake, who probably thought it had waited too long the last time I opened the door, almost flew off the window-sill onto the floor and came straight at me in a blur of speed. Wow! I had intended to calmly pin it to the floor with the back of the rake-head, but now I frantically chopped and chopped as it came at me. I broke the rake handle in my frenzy, but I managed to kill the poor damn snake in the process. Then, with the action over, my workman volunteer entered the house to remove the mangled remains of the snake on his shovel, just as the television reporters arrived.

It took me some time to calm down after my ordeal, and I was still shaking as I rode away soon after. As the lady of the house – hair done and make-up hastily applied – posed with the dead snake and my now confident workman volunteer for the benefit of the television cameras. I doubt whether either of them shared the nightmares I later had about my close encounter with that damn snake.

CHAPTER TWELVE

A Well Collapse and Domestics

"You won't leave me here Mister... Will you?" That simple poignant remark made to me over thirty three years ago by a very frightened twelve year old boy we were trying to rescue from a dry-well cave-in, sticks in my memory. It still brings a shiver to my old bones as I think of the situation the poor kid was in.

It was late afternoon on what had been a hot summer's day in February 1963. I was on the 3pm to 11pm shift at the Innaloo Police station sorting out files to attend to on my evening run, when the phone rang.

"My brother's buried. Hurry! Dad's try'n to dig him out but the sand keeps goin' in on him!" There was panic in the young voice as the words spilled out.

"Steady now. We'll be there in a jiffy" I said reassuringly. "Where is your brother and what's happened?"

"In a hole in the backyard. We were diggin' the dry-well and it fell in on him and Dad can't get him out!"

"Okay. We're on the way. What's the address?"

"253 Ravenscar Street (Doubleview)."

"We're on our way. Don't worry we'll get him out okay."

I quickly alerted my boss, Sergeant Charlie Watts, (who was at home in the adjacent Police quarters) and grabbing a couple of shovels I was off on the station motorbike combination within a minute of the call, accompanied by a police trainee who was at the station on a temporary posting for work experience. I knew the District well and was able to reach the address within minutes. The boys father, Laurie Elliott, quickly guided us to the back of the house. There in the backyard, close to what remained of an area partially covered with cement slabs, was an almost funnel shaped hole about 6 feet deep. A ladder used in the hole and now buried deep in the loose soft sand was propped against and partially supporting the one remaining portion of sand-wall.

Behind and beneath the ladder, facing the wall and buried up to the top of his shoulders in loose sand, was the head of the boy. He had a piece of cloth over his head and was attempting to breathe through a garden hose. I spoke to him telling him who we were and, with more confidence than I felt, that we'd have him out in no time. Although obviously frightened the boy wasn't panicking and seemed to cheer up a bit when he knew police help had arrived.

Mr Elliott told me that his two boys, Murray (aged twelve) assisted by his elder brother Ken (aged fourteen), had spent most of the day digging a hole for a new dry-well for the family's septic tank system. Murray was at the bottom of the 9 feet deep hole, squaring the sides in readiness for the curved brick segments when the sides of the hole collapsed on him. He arrived home to check on the boys only seconds later and desperately tried to free Murray, but the bone dry sand ran like water. As fast as he tried to dig the faster the sand ran in. The mere weight of his body on the 45 degree slope of the collapsed well caused more sand to flow down on to Murray.

We quickly isolated the fragile area around the hole. It was obvious that if the small remaining section of wall collapsed the trapped boy would die. Sergeant Watts, who was followed shortly after by two other policemen from Scarborough station arrived to assist as Laurie Elliott and I quickly gathered shoring material to hold back the sand.

It had to be a very delicate operation. A sheet of corrugated iron was edged down the wall in front of Murray's head and secured with timber. But digging him out became a lengthy and very difficult exercise because of the fragile surface around the hole and the dry sand. As soon as anyone stepped near the hole, or worse still into the hole, the flow of sand started again submerging Murray further.

We had to have someone in the hole to guide the shoring into position. I lay on my stomach and wriggled head-first down the slope while Sergeant Watts held my legs. Although there was some slippage of the surface it was not as great as it would have been had I been standing, as the flatness of my body created less pressure.

It was like trying to dig a trench in a sand dune. At first I started with a small shovel, passing half shovel-fulls back to Charlie Watts but this was too awkward. Most of the fine dry sand ran off the shovel before we could get it to the surface. Then someone passed me down a kitchen pot which was much better. Progress was agonizingly slow and as I carefully gained a little space other members of the rescue team forced whatever shoring material they could muster into position beside me.

There were other complications as well. We were talking and joking with young Murray as the work progressed and I learnt from him (and could see as I got closer) that as the well collapsed behind him the weight of the sand pushed the ladder forward, forcing him onto his knees against the other side of the hole. His bent legs now held him like a hook in the sand and he was actually kneeling on the edge of the shovel he'd been using. Additionally, as the sand poured in many of the paving slabs from around the opening came with it, which was both a blessing and an encumbrance, for while they had slowed some of the sand flow the slabs now obstructed the digging. We managed to get a rope around Murray under his arms and the rescuers above maintained a slight pressure on the rope ready to pull him clear once I could free his legs.

He was a brave little kid. Although he was frightened and in some pain from the shovel edge cutting into his knee, he did as he was told; didn't move about or attempt to claw himself free as I slowly removed small pot-full after small pot-full of sand from around him.

Suddenly part of our make-shift shoring slipped (no wonder with all the activity above) and loose sand started to flow back into the area around Murray and me, as the rescuers above desperately shoved and pushed other material into place trying to stop the flow. It was "a bit hairy" for a minute or two, believe me.

Sergeant Watts, who was further up the slope, quickly took hold of my legs again and said, "Don't worry. If it (the sand-wall) collapses I'll jerk you free"

My head was only a foot or two away from Murray's, who was still firmly held by his bent legs. As the Sergeant spoke Murray turned his face towards me and we made eye contact. As the sand trickled in around us he asked, in a quiet little voice, "You won't leave me here Mister...Will you?"

His poignant question sent a cold shiver up my spine, which returns again now as I write. For although the danger to me was relatively minor, had the makeshift shoring given way a huge amount of loose sand would have poured in, quickly covering the bottom of the funnel-shaped pit – bringing certain death to the trapped boy.

"No way mate!" I replied with a grin, "We're goin' out of here together. And we're almost there now."

And so the slow removal of sand continued for about another ten minutes or so until I could see that only an inch or two of sand now held the boys legs. Then very carefully, with the rescuers above helping to raise him with the rope around his chest, we got Murray to stand up. He was free and to the cheers of all present we quickly helped him up out of the hole. Our team effort had been successful and a young life had been saved. It was a good feeling.

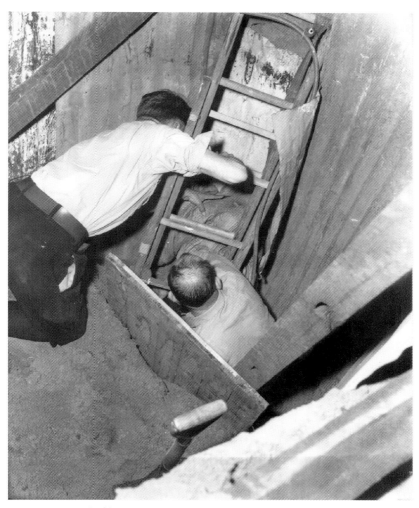

Sgt C Watts (left) and Constable R. Primrose down well with back to camera talking to the trapped boy Murray. (Photo courtesy of The West Australian.)

In December 1996 I spoke with Murray Elliott again. Now aged forty-six, happily married with four sons aged between twenty-five and fourteen, Murray runs a successful drafting service business at Duncraig. It was great to meet him again after all these years, and we spent a pleasant hour or two discussing the circumstances of his "near death" experience as a twelve year old boy.

For me and the other policemen involved, although Murray's rescue gave us great satisfaction we were really just doing our job. But it meant much more to Murray – a precious young life that was nearly "snuffed out" was given the opportunity to reach adulthood. Although I've always felt good about being involved in Murray's rescue, to meet him again now and learn of his successes in life, makes our efforts on that almost fatal day seem even more worthwhile.

*   *   *   *   *

Although the initial staff allocation for Innaloo was two (ie the Sergeant and me), the work-load certainly warranted more. So as time went on staff numbers were gradually increased until we had three constables and the Sergeant. Early in 1966 our transport was finally upgraded to a motor car, a two door Ford Cortina sedan with two way radio. It was quite a luxury after the motorcycle combination. About this time also, Sergeant Watts was promoted and moved on, to be replaced as officer in charge by Sergeant Athol Baker, who was likewise an experienced and competent officer.

One of the work problems I remember most about Innaloo was the ongoing incidence of domestic violence, and the reluctance of the female victims to take action. It almost makes my blood boil when critics blame the police for failing to help women who have been assaulted by their husband, (or as the popular term is these days, "their partner"). I have personally – and know for a fact that other police do the same – almost pleaded with some women in such situations to accept police assistance to charge their assailant. But no. They refuse and it's generally, "Next time I will. Just warn him. And next time I'll take action." And so the charade goes on, with police returning on a regular basis to offer the same advice or deliver the same lecture about what "might" happen next time.

Prior to 1994, when amendments to the Evidence Act changed the situation, a woman could not be compelled to give evidence against her husband. Although if she chose to, the Courts accepted her as a competent witness. Therefore, in most domestic assault cases, police could not take action unless the wife agreed to give evidence. Recent statistics (1997) show that 50% of all murders in Western Australia can be directly related to domestic violence.

It's extremely frustrating for Police, and can be quite dangerous as many police attending a domestic have been killed or seriously injured. But you have to respond no matter how trivial or useless you think it may be when it's one of your "regulars". You just never know what you're going to find when you get there. Like the night I attended one of our regular pay-night domestic situations. He was drunk as usual and had come home almost broke. They argued and he threatened to kill himself (a common emotional blackmail ploy). But this time he had taken it one step further. His wife told me she found him standing on top of their washing machine, a rope tied around his neck and the other end tied to an over-head beam. She cut the rope and phoned the police station. When I went out the back to the laundry, there he was balancing unsteadily on the washing machine trying to tie the two ends of the cut rope together.

So I helped him! .. Only joking, but I must confess I thought about it briefly. I got him down (before he fell and broke his neck) and after I talked to him for a while it seemed to me he was not only suffering from too much to drink, but also from a psychiatric disorder. It was too risky to leave him to his own devices (his wife could do nothing with him) so I apprehended him under the provisions of the then Mental Health Act for his own safety. When it was later established that his mental instability was the result of his excessive drinking, he was sentenced by the Court to a period of compulsory treatment under the provisions of the Inebriates Act.

But so often there is very little you can do. For example the crazy domestic relationship between a big raw-boned Scotsman, we'll call "Jock", and his bird-like nervous little wife "Dorothy", demonstrates the frustration I felt about having to continually deal with people of their ilk. It was rumoured that Jock and Dorothy first met while both were in hospital receiving treatment for psychiatric problems (I can well believe it), and they later married.

Why they ever stayed together I'll never know. Big Jock was a regular drinker at the local watering hole, the Morris Hotel. He was no trouble in the pub but every three of four weeks, when he got home late she would nag him, there'd be a blue, and he would slap her around. There were no split lips or black eyes, but Dorothy's face would be red and bruised all over from Jock's open handed slaps. Innaloo Police, or police from elsewhere if we were not available, attended domestics at their home on a regular basis. And it always seemed my luck to be on duty when the call came in. It was crazy. I got to know both of them well over the years and the scenario rarely changed.

As I stopped the car (earlier the motorbike) in the street outside their home, Jock would come out to greet me like I was there on a social visit. He wasn't an unlikable bloke, in spite of his cruelty to Dorothy. He'd say (something like) "G'day mate. You've come to give me a little lecture again have you?" or "Those bloody nosy neighbours of mine been ringin' you up again, have they?" Disturbed by Dorothy's screams, the neighbours often phoned us. I'd usually find Dorothy in the bedroom or bathroom, crying and nursing her bruised face, and we'd go through the whole process over again. Although once or twice she did take some advice and seek help from the Women Police and Social Welfare people, it came to nothing. All she wanted was for me to tell Jock to stop hitting her. She would agree to nothing else. So I would go through the pantomime again, trying to remain serious or control my anger as Jock treated the matter like the sick joke it was. But there was nothing else I could do.

Of course sometimes the assault is far more violent and police involvement seen as interference and strongly opposed, as it was in the domestic between "Yvonne" and her husband.

I was working on my own in the office on a Saturday afternoon when the phone rang. A dramatic female voice said, "Come quickly. A woman is screaming next door and I am frightened she's being murdered."

I quickly got the caller's name and the address where the screams had come from (less than a kilometre from the station) and I was away in the Police car. These days you would always arrange a back-up when called to an incident like this, but back then there were few police available for such a rapid response. Where time was crucial you went on your own and did the best you could. I parked the car and pounded on the front door of the house, identifying myself and demanding entrance. The door was half opened and I was confronted by a man inside. He was wearing a white long sleeve shirt and I could see it was splattered with fresh blood.

"What do YOU want?" he demanded aggressively.

"I've had a report of a woman's screams coming from this house. What's going on?" I asked.

"It was my wife. We had a fight and I hit her. It's over. It's got nothing to do with you."

"Maybe, but I want to speak to the lady to see she is alright."

"She is okay. It's got nothing to do with you." He was starting to close the door.

"Hold on" I said, as I blocked the door with my foot to stop it closing, "Just let me in to see her and if she's alright I'll go."

"No." He tried to force the door shut. "You're not coming in here without a warrant."

I was not convinced that what he said was true, and there was no time to get a warrant. In circumstances like this, where a police officer has a genuine belief that a life may be in danger, common law prevails and a warrant to enter premises is not necessary. I hit the door hard with my shoulder and forced my way past him into the house, as he shouted abuse and threats at me. I warned him what to expect if he tried to obstruct me and quickly located the lady involved in the main bedroom.

Then, what a shock! It was Yvonne, a woman I knew well as a fellow member of a mixed choral group to which I belonged. I hardly recognised her at first. She was sitting on the side of the bed sobbing; her swollen face swathed in a wet towel, bleeding from the nose and cuts to her lips. She had obviously been savagely beaten. I spoke to Yvonne and confirmed she had no injuries other than the cuts on her face. While the husband continued to shout threats at me I offered protection and quietly tried to persuade her to come with me, at least for medical attention. But she declined, thanking me for my concern and offer of help. She confirmed what her husband said had taken place. They argued. He hit her and it was over. I felt quite strongly about the needless brutality inflicted on the poor woman, and I almost wished the bloke would take a poke at me so I could justify giving him a bit of his own medicine.

There was nothing else I could do. I left the house a few minutes later to the accompanying threats of the irate husband, who said he intended to sue me for assaulting him, invading his home and interfering in his domestic affairs. I later advised the concerned neighbour that Yvonne was in no further danger, then wrote the incident up in the Station Occurrences. That should have been the end of it, but a couple of weeks later Yvonne's husband came to see me at the station. He was a very different bloke to the one I had dealt with before. He said he had come to apologize to me personally for the way he acted. He didn't say what caused the argument, but said it was the first time he had ever lost his temper and assaulted his wife during their many years of marriage, and was thoroughly ashamed of himself for acting as he did. He said that Yvonne had forgiven him and he hoped that I would also. I believe his remorse was genuine and accepted his apology. What he did disgusted me but I admired his guts for trying to make amends.

And it seems he succeeded. Perhaps their marriage was strong enough to survive, for after their "one off" violent domestic, as far as I am aware there was never any further police involvement. There are always a lot of "one off" domestics, and they vary in degree of complexity and violence. But it is the "regulars", the pests that want to involve the police every time they have some trivial argument or who won't do anything to correct their problem, that police find most annoying.

When it comes to "pests" I have dealt with, "Jack" the PMG (now Telstra) technician and his shrew of a wife, just about take the cake. Over a period of about six months or so you could almost bet on getting called to a domestic between Jack and his wife at least once every two or three weeks. There was no real violence in their disputes. I never could work out what it was all about, but there was lots of shouting and screaming and pathetic suicidal threats. Jack drank a bit but not really to excess. They had a well maintained home at Innaloo, and obviously enjoyed a good standard of living. But when the stops were out they threw small household items and matched each other in their level of petty insults, abuse and threats. It was usually the wife who phoned, but trying to sort out their problem or who was to blame was almost impossible.

Then one night I received a telephone call from Central Police communications that Jack's wife – who was temporarily separated from him and living with her mother

149

– had phoned to advise that Jack had taken an over-dose of drugs in an attempt to take his life. It was stated that Jack, who was at their Innaloo address, had telephoned his wife at her mother's to tell her he'd decided to "end it all", and had taken an over-dose. Central Police had directed an ambulance to Jack's home and I was to attend and assist.

As I arrived in the street where Jack lived I saw the ambulance moving off in the other direction, so I contacted Police Communications (VKI) on my car radio and asked for an update on the situation from the ambulance crew. Through their link-up between ambulance and Police communications, the ambulance crew advised that Jack was still at his home. He was conscious when they arrived but refused to leave with them. They were unsure if he had taken any drugs but said he had obviously been drinking. Great! Now I had to deal with the pest.

I found Jack lying half asleep (unconscious?) on a single bed on the back verandah of the house. I roused him and got him into the kitchen, trying to find out if he really had taken anything this time – as he had threatened to do so many times in the past. He seemed as though he was drunk but I couldn't get him to tell me if or what he had taken that was likely to harm him. He just went on and on with his usual garbage about how terrible his wife treated him and how he was going to show her this time by "knocking himself off".

He said, "It's no good waitin' around. I'm goin' to do it this time. I'll show her. She'll be sorry. Neither you nor anyone else is going to stop me."

I was really fed up with him by this. I'd heard him make similar threats so many times before. I angrily shot back at him "Knock yourself off? I wish you would, then I'd be done with you. I could write up a report and it would be over. But no, you pathetic B... you're just a bloody pest. You haven't got the guts to do it. All you ever do is go on and on talking about it."

I must have shocked him for he paused in his diatribe

and said, "You don't think I'll do it do you?"

"No." I said, "I don't."

We were standing on opposite sides of the large kitchen table, which was surrounded by several chairs. Jack had a large glass of beer in his hand. Suddenly, before I could get to him, he quickly withdrew his other hand from his trouser pocket, stuffed a mixture of barbiturate capsules and tablets into his mouth and sloshed them down with the beer. I managed to grab a couple of capsules and tablets that missed his mouth, but I had no idea how many he swallowed (or if he had taken any previously). Although I tried to get him to regurgitate the drugs or come with me in the police car, he resisted until the substances he had taken took affect and he collapsed in a heap on the floor.

I had to act quickly but with Jack's size (equal at least to mine) and his limp condition it became quite a problem. I had to drag him along the ground, then pull him into the rear of the police car – where he lay sprawled unconscious on the seat as I sped off to Casualty Section at Royal Perth Hospital. He was revived, of course – the stomach pump is a very effective piece of equipment – and admitted to Hospital for observation. When I was speaking with medical staff at R.P.H and afterwards as I completed my report I naturally didn't elaborate too much on what happened at the house.

It later became apparent that Jack himself didn't know the full story. A couple of weeks after the incident I was working in the station on my own one afternoon, when Jack walked in.

"Constable," he said, "I understand it was you that attended my home a few weeks back when I made an attempt on my life."

"Yes. That's right Jack." I said.

"Well," he said, extending his hand, "I'd like to thank you and shake you by the hand. I understand that if it hadn't been for your prompt action I would have died."

"That's okay Jack" I sheepishly replied as we shook hands, "I was only doing my job. But thanks anyway."

CHAPTER THIRTEEN

Justice – You be the Judge

As a routine part of their duty, Police whilst on patrol, are always on the look-out for stolen vehicles and should also check on vehicles parked (perhaps abandoned) in odd places or, in what seems to be "unusual" circumstances. In this manner offenders are sometimes caught on the job and charged with crimes they may otherwise get away with.

I remember one situation like this, where the two young offenders I arrested must have believed they were really unlucky to be caught, as the scheme they were operating seemed almost foolproof.

Before the present Karrinyup shopping complex opened in September 1973, temporary facilities were provided by a number of small businesses housed in a barn-shaped shed, built for the purpose at the north west corner of Karrinyup Road and Francis Avenue. This little shopping centre with its small parking area was isolated by an expanse of virgin land behind it to the west and to the north along Francis Avenue, where the current shopping complex now stands. As I live at Karrinyup I regularly drove past this shopping centre on my way to and from work at Innaloo. It was also a location we (Innaloo Police) included in our routine patrols.

Late one night I found a car parked in the shopping

centre car park. As it was unusual to see a single vehicle parked in this isolated area at that time of night, I examined the car closely and checked to see if it was stolen. But it was not on the "hot list". Its doors were all locked, and there was no sign of forced entry or other damage. The next day the car was gone, only to reappear parked as before a night or two later. It was quite strange, as over the next week or two the car would be there some nights, even parked for a day before it was gone again. There was nothing illegal about it being parked where it was, it was just unusual. As my shifts rotated, and the weeks went by, I didn't notice whether the car was there or not – there was no reason to keep checking. Then at least a month or two after I first noticed the car there was a re-play of the scenario, only this time it was a different car. Perhaps it is a business person (I thought) who doesn't want the neighbours to know, or someone keeping a love tryst. But why a different car? Something was not right. It puzzled me.

Then finally, by sheer chance, the pieces came together and the puzzle was solved. I was driving past the shopping centre in the police car on my way home for Sunday lunch. I had seen the mystery car parked there earlier that morning as I drove past on my way to work. It seemed as though it had been there overnight and it was parked in a reversed position against the kerb. The car was still parked as I had seen it earlier, but now I saw two youths walking towards it as though they were about to drive it away. Uh hah! An opportunity to satisfy my curiosity. I did a "U" turn and entered the car-park as the youths unlocked the car and got in. Then as I drew near I heard the engine start so I stopped the police car directly across the front of their vehicle, to prevent them moving off before I could speak to them.

As I got out of the police car and approached the driver's side door, the driver revved the engine impatiently indicating that he wanted to move off. But he had nowhere to go with the rear wheels of the car against the kerb and my car parked directly in front. His window was up so I knocked on it and told him to wind it down as I wanted to speak to him, and he did so. As I still had no firm suspicion about them or the car (I was driven mainly by my own curiosity) I leant down to speak with the driver at eye-level and said "Tell me, why do you park the vehicle here?"

"What do you mean?" he said.

"Why do you leave it here all the time?"

"We don't. We only parked it here a while ago."

As he spoke I looked a little closer into the car. The driver had engaged gear and kept his foot on the depressed clutch as he revved the motor. His left hand held the emergency brake ready for quick release, and his legs and arms were shaking with tension. A glance at the passenger – now trying to conceal the socks he had on his hands – confirmed my growing suspicion that all was not what it seemed to be. Then as the passenger suddenly panicked and tried to open his door I said, "Like hell you did", as I quickly reached across the driver and grabbed him by the arm to stop his escape. At this the driver also broke shouting, "Okay! Okay! You've got us. It's a stolen car." (A stolen car? how could it be a stolen car? It had been parked there on and off for days. I'd checked a couple of times and it wasn't on the hot list.)

The commotion attracted the attention of an off-duty detective who was leaving the nearby shops, and he came over and helped me. When we took the two youths back to the Police station and questioned them, they admitted they were responsible for the theft of several vehicles over a period of about six months. One of them worked for a large car wrecking firm and had ready access to car parts. Their scheme was to steal a vehicle, remove and destroy the number plates, then fit the plates, ignition switch and door lock taken from a similar vehicle in the wrecking yard. The disguised stolen vehicle could then be used for several weeks without detection. When they finally abandoned a stolen vehicle they removed and destroyed the false plates, so they couldn't be traced to the wreckers, before stealing another car and repeating the process.

It was a clever almost foolproof scheme that only came unstuck because a suburban policeman sought to satisfy his curiosity. Perhaps that strange factor, "intuition," played a part in their capture and helped to ensure Justice was done?

*   *   *   *   *

People often speak of a policeman's intuition, that inexplicable sixth sense he may be able to call on when investigating a crime. But believe me there are not too many "Sherlock Holmes'" about, and most offences are only solved after meticulous investigation and the compilation of evidence. Obviously the experience you gain in dealing with people and assessing situations helps, but intuition is an aid, not an end all, although sometimes it does help to point you in the right direction. I guess it may have helped me catch the sad young Doubleview "snow dropper" – a person who steals clothing left to dry on a clothes-line.

Over a period of several months Doubleview, and parts of Innaloo, was plagued with snow dropping. It was always items of women's under-wear; stockings, nightwear, bras, panties and bathers. We received a dozen or so reports, and, as we later learnt, at least the same number of offences went unreported. Persons who chose to report their loss, did so at either the Innaloo or Scarborough police stations, and a "M.O." report would be completed.

An M.O. (Modus Operandi) is a standard report form police use to record details of an offence, the complainant's particulars and other relevant data. Several copies of an M.O. are made and distributed for either information, attention, or for inquiry in the area where the offence occurred. Therefore, in relation to the Doubleview snow dropping, we received the Scarborough M.O. reports for inquiry also.

I had a number of these petty snow dropping M.O.s

155

for attention, and while I sometimes made a token effort to gain a lead, in most instances they were dead-end inquiries. So generally I just waited a respectable time before formally notifying the complainant that my inquiries had been unsuccessful. After all can you imagine trying to find the culprit responsible for the theft of a pair of stockings or such-like, from a back-yard clothes-line? Anyway I did my bit of "P.R." to keep the customers happy, as I called on the ladies who had reported their loss to reassure them how diligently we had tried to track down the villain responsible. Then I very nearly got caught out one afternoon as I delivered my standard spiel to a lady named Mrs Jones (not her real name) who had had her red bikini bathers stolen (reported at Scarborough).

I started to tell Mrs Jones that, although "all possible inquiries had been made etc etc.." when I noticed she was giving me a bit of a cynical grin. She obviously didn't believe me. So as I wound up the notification I deleted the personal reference, saying instead "police have been unable to locate the offender or your stolen bathers."

"Tell me Constable," an amused Mrs Jones asked, "Just what inquiry did you make."

"Well to be honest, Mrs Jones," I said, "I personally haven't made any inquiries. I'm really only here to tell you we haven't found your bathers. Why do you ask?"

"Because," she said, "the day after I reported that my bathers had been stolen, my neighbour two doors up told me that she found young Claude Stanley (not his real name) acting suspiciously in her backyard late one afternoon a few days before. When she challenged him he claimed he was looking for a tap to get a drink of water, which is quite ridiculous because he only lives up the street."

Mrs Jones went on to say that she passed this information on to Scarborough Police, nominating young Stanley, a student at Scarborough High School, as a possible suspect for the theft of her bathers. Obviously the information was never passed on to us at Innaloo. It was the lead I needed, and I told Mrs Jones I would check it right away. It was mid-afternoon so I went directly to the High School and asked the Deputy Headmaster for permission to speak with the boy in his office. In answer to the Deputy's query I briefly explained that Stanley was a possible suspect for the theft of women's clothing. He was astounded. He said he couldn't believe it; Claude Stanley was possibly the brightest boy at the school; an exceptional student with an IQ bordering on the genius.

I insisted that I still needed to question him, so the Deputy sent a message for Stanley to come to the office. A short time later Claude Stanley, a gangling serious faced youth of about 15, was ushered into the office and introduced to me by the Deputy. As soon as I saw him, and before he even spoke, some sixth sense told me Stanley was responsible for the snow-dropping offences. So, dispensing with the preliminaries , I simply said, "Claude, where is the red bikini you stole from Mrs Jones' clothes-line a few weeks ago?"

Without hesitation, he quietly replied, "They're under my pillow at home."

"And what about all the other women's things you've been stealing during the past few weeks?" I followed on.

"They're in my room or in my bed."

The Deputy Headmaster was now frantically signalling me that we must talk in private. So we excused ourselves and left the room.

"Good grief!" he exclaimed, as soon as the door was closed, "How did you know he was responsible? What happens now?"

I explained my reasons, and that subject to interviewing him more fully in the presence of his parents, Claude would be arrested and charged with theft. I also said that I believed the boy's strange conduct suggested he may be a sexual deviant who really needed psychiatric help to correct his problem, and that a Court order was essential so the Child Welfare Department could monitor his treatment and progress.

The Deputy, who agreed that Claude probably did

need psychiatric help, tried hard to persuade me that there may be an alternative way for Claude to get psychiatric treatment. He was very concerned that a conviction for theft may have a serious effect on Claude's future. I wished there was another way, but there wasn't. I had also learnt from him in the course of our conversation that Claude lived alone with his mother, who took little interest in his schooling, and that his father, an ex-policeman, no longer lived with them and had no contact with his son. Although I knew there was no alternative, to pacify the Deputy Headmaster I contacted the Child Welfare Dept and spoke at length with the Social Worker responsible for our area. He also conferred with the Deputy by phone, assuring him that to ensure the boy did receive appropriate help it was essential that he be charged and appear before the Children's Court so that an Order for Treatment could be obtained.

After confirming with Claude that his mother was there, I took him home in the Police car, and what a tragic unhealthy situation I found there. Claude's mother was a small bird-like dowdy woman of limited intelligence. It was a hot humid day, and all outer doors and windows on the small Housing Commission rental home were closed. The air was stale and a strong sour smell permeated every room. The house seemed like it hadn't been aired, or cleaned or tidied for months, and Claude's bedroom was probably the worst. It was almost like a dingo pen. The bed linen and coverings were filthy, they looked like they had never been changed or washed. I've seen derelicts' camps in the bush with cleaner sleeping arrangements. Scattered about the bedroom were the (now soiled) items of women's under-wear that Claude admitted he had stolen from clothes-lines in the area. It was really sickening. How this poor young kid could have lived in such an environment and done so well academically is a mystery.

I did what I had to do and the rest was up to the Child Welfare Department. I wonder how things finally worked out for young Claude, anything had to be better than the way he was heading. I just hope that, after proper treatment, he was able to go on and make good use of his brilliance. But I will always think of him as the sad young Doubleview snow-dropper.

*   *   *   *   *

Working for a number of years at Innaloo Police station, I came to know many people well. And I saw a lot of young people go off the rails for one reason or another. I often had a word with a kid who was just coming under notice, to warn him where he may be heading. Responsible parents also occasionally sought our help in matters of family discipline, and brought their unruly child to the police station for a talk. But sadly too few really took much notice, and I later saw many graduate, as they progressed through their early teens to adulthood, from petty theft to house-breaking, car stealing and major crime – wasting so many precious years in gaol. It has always made me feel sad to see young people who have been blessed with a sound mind and body, waste their life like this. And while the old adage "you can't put an old head on young shoulders" may well apply in most instances, some parents are at least equally to blame for their child's downfall, through lack of discipline, over-indulgence or simply because they plant and develop an anti-authority, anti-police attitude in their child's mind at an early age. I recall the parents of one seventeen year old Doubleview youth – particularly the mother – who surely must have lived to regret the end result of the anti-police attitude they encouraged in their son. It happened like this.

I received a telephone message from Maylands Police that a couple of nights before, a youth aged sixteen had been assaulted outside a dance hall in Maylands. It was alleged he was standing outside the hall waiting for some friends when a passing car suddenly stopped, and a male passenger, who was aged about twenty, got out and punched him in the face. Fortunately, apart from a blooded nose, the young man was not seriously injured. He claimed he didn't know his assailant, and did nothing to provoke the assault. The number of the car had been taken at the time, and a check of records showed it to be registered in the name of Charles James Wilson (not his real name) of Huntriss Street Doubleview. I was asked to interview Wilson about the incident and try to learn the name of the assailant.

When I arrived at the address, near the south end of Huntriss Street, I saw that the house was a large modern multi-level building. It seemed the Wilson's were obviously "well-to-do" people. Answering the door-bell, Mrs Wilson said that Charles James Wilson (the registered owner of the car), was her seventeen year old son and that he was at home. I explained to Mrs Wilson that I wanted to speak to Charles about an incident involving the use of his car a few nights earlier. She invited me in, called her son to join us in the lounge, and remained there at my request while I questioned him.

Charles, who was a bit over-awed by the whole thing, confirmed the sequence of events up to the time he stopped his car outside the dance hall and his passenger got out. But when I sought more information from him, and asked for the name of his passenger, Mrs Wilson quickly cut in and took over, "Surely Constable you don't really expect Charles to tell tales on his friend, do you?"

Tell tales? I hadn't expected this. The woman appeared to be intelligent and well educated. I'd expected a more responsible attitude.

"Mrs Wilson," I said, "I don't think that's the way we should look at it. This is a serious criminal offence, not some petty children's back-yard squabble we're talking about. What I am trying to find out is why this man, who Charles agrees was a passenger in his car, got out and punched an apparently innocent sixteen year old boy in the face. Perhaps there was a reason, but at present we don't know. Charles was there, he could tell me what happened and give me the name of his passenger – who is said to be aged about twenty. There is no suggestion that Charles has done anything wrong, but I do need his help to find out what happened."

"No. Charles has always been taught not to tell tales," she firmly replied, "And it's his friend you're now asking him to tell on. I don't think he should."

Her attitude really surprised me. She had completely taken over and was not giving Charles himself a chance to express an opinion. I could see by his body language that Charles was not an assertive person, and was probably grateful for the "mother hen" role she was adopting. But I wasn't prepared to give in that easily, so I modified my approach and I said, "Doesn't it concern you at all Mrs Wilson that, because Charles is protecting this man who it seems acted like a thug, he is likely to get away with it and could thump some other innocent kid in the future? Is this the sort of man you really want your son to associate with?"

"We can't tell Charles who he can be friends with."

"How would you feel if Charles was bashed in this manner? Wouldn't you expect the police to find the person responsible?"

"Of course I would. That's your job."

"It may be our job, but we're not psychic. Without help from the general public there is very little we can do." On and on the discussion continued, but I failed to persuade her in the slightest. As for Charles, he simply said nothing.

I had done the best I could so I finally gave up. I said, "Well Mrs Wilson if the situation is ever reversed, and your Charles is the victim, I hope you both remember our discussion here today, and don't blame the police if we can't find the offender. Also, Charles, if this thug you're now protecting with your mother's blessing, is typical of the company you keep it won't be long before you're in real trouble yourself." (I would have bet money on it.)

It was like water off a duck's back. I thanked them

for their time and left, later advising Police at Maylands that I had been unable to gain any information that would help them in their inquiries.

Oh yes I did make contact with Mr Wilson. I spoke to him later by phone at his business premises, in a last ditch attempt before advising Maylands Police of the negative result. It was fruitless. He said he wouldn't interfere, and that he shared his wife's view-point.

Time passed, and a few months later I learnt that Charles had been charged and convicted of receiving stolen property. Then possibly 12 months after the Maylands incident, I heard he had been arrested and charged with complicity in a number of armed robbery offences (apparently Charles was the driver of the get-away car). His parents were probably devastated when he was convicted and sentenced to imprisonment, but I wonder if they were ever prepared to accept part of the blame.

*   *   *   *   *

The primary role of police within our judicial system is to thoroughly investigate matters in their area of responsibility; to then assess the available evidence, and decide whether to dismiss, caution, or prosecute. If a decision is made to prosecute, the police have a duty to properly present all available evidence to the Court. From that point on the guilt or otherwise of the person charged is solely a matter for the Court to decide. The end result (either way) should not concern the police. However we policemen are human too, and while you may keep reminding yourself that the end result is not your concern, the Court process can often be traumatic and the end result disappointing or (on the other hand) quite exhilarating when justice against all odds is seen to be done.

A particular case I remember demonstrates the point. It was only a relatively minor drunk-driving charge, but the personal stress that it caused me, and the relief I felt when it was finally over was way out of proportion to the importance of the charge involved. Before relating the story, let me first set the scene.

The Innaloo Police District had its fair share of people who drank too much and drove their vehicles while drunk. Many were stopped, assessed, cautioned or charged by police. For some reason it seemed I attracted suspected drunk drivers like flies to a honey pot, and although I cautioned far more than I ever charged I came to be viewed as a bit of a "bogey-man" by the local blokes who over-indulged.

Until the breathalyser came into use in this state, the courts relied mainly on the visual evidence of police. And even after the breathalyser became law in 1966, it was still two or three years before a suspected drunk driver had to also supply a sample of his breath at the scene for a "preliminary test". So that was the situation that existed during most of my time at Innaloo, I relied on my personal experience to assess a suspect's condition and used my discretion on whether to charge them or not.

Although most persons who are charged with drunken driving plead guilty when they appear before the Court of Petty Sessions, in those days most "not guilty" pleas were vigorously defended. And as the result nearly always depended on the credibility of the arresting officer, as such, you expected to bear the brunt of the defence counsel's attack.

However in the case I am about to relate, everything seemed to get blown out of proportion, because of the particular person involved and the general circumstances of the case.

It was about 10 pm on a wet and blustery Saturday night. One of those nights when I was glad to stay in the office, hoping the phone wouldn't ring before I finished my shift. And, as always seems to be the case, the phone did ring. It was Police communications.

"We've just had a call from a Mr Lyall Offin, of 600 Dwyer street Doubleview (not his real name or address), who said that as he was reversing his car out of his driveway a short time ago, he bumped a light pole in the street bringing down the power lines. He has called the S.E.C. (now Western Power) but because of the severe conditions tonight, they won't be able to get there for at least an hour. Mr Offin is concerned about the danger and asks that police attend until the S.E.C. can get there."

It was raining when I arrived and parked near the address given. I could see sparks coming from the live wires as they contacted the wet road, and a number of people walking about the area. As I got out of the Police car Mr Offin came over and introduced himself. He clasped me around the shoulders and started to guide me in the direction of the fallen wires. He breath smelt strongly of beer and he leant on me for support, addressing me as "my boy" as he sought to show me where the live wires lay. He was obviously drunk and in no condition to be wandering about near live power lines, let alone driving a car.

My immediate priority was the safety of people in the area, so I removed myself from Offin's clasp, and said, "Okay Mr Offin I can look after things now. But I want you and the others (he had told me they were his children and their friends) to get back in the house. I don't want anyone wandering about in the street with these power lines down."

"Now just a minute," he said, "you think that I was driving the car, don't you?"

Well.. (I thought).. that's apparently what you said when you phoned the Police to ask for help, so I said, "Yes, I do."

"Well you're wrong," Offin said, "My wife was driving the car when it hit the pole. I'm too drunk to be driving. If it was me you'd have to arrest me, wouldn't you?"

I quickly assessed the situation and decided it was appropriate to exercise my discretion. Offin was obviously a responsible citizen; he had phoned both the S.E.C. and police to alert them of the danger; it was a shocking night;

the power pole was fairly close to the kerb and (it could be argued) not easy to avoid. Although it was pretty obvious he was the driver I had little proof, so I decided to go along with the charade, as the fallen power-lines were of greater importance. So I said, "You're right, I would. So I'm glad it was your wife who was driving. But that doesn't alter what I first said – would you please take your kids and get off the street away from these live wires."

In a short time they were gone and I had the street to myself. I parked the police car in the centre of the road with its hazard lights flashing (in those days suburban police cars had only an illuminated Police sign), and using a broom (which one of Offin's kids got for me) I pulled the live wires clear of the bitumen and placed them near the base of the power poles. Then I settled down to wait in the Police car for the S.E.C. to arrive.

It then dawned on me that this, i.e. power lines brought down as the result of a car-v-power pole collision, had to be dealt with as a traffic accident, minor though it was. Offin had said his wife was driving, so I would need her Driver's License particulars for the accident report. Although I had little doubt that Offin would have, by now, alerted his wife to the fact that he had told me she was the driver of the car, I didn't want to stuff up his story by having her deny that she was in fact the driver. So when she came to the door in answer to my knock, I gave her no chance. I said, "Mrs Offin you husband said you were driving the car when it hit the power pole... (this was said as a statement not as a question, as I continued on without giving her much of a chance to contradict me) ...but although it's only a minor accident I do have to get your Driver's License particulars so I can complete a Traffic Accident Report."

It was a "wink wink nudge nudge" sort of a situation. I was genuinely trying to do the right thing because of the overall circumstances, and Mrs Offin cottoned on straight away. She said, "Yes that's right Constable. Please come in while I get my license for you."

165

She showed me into the kitchen where her husband was now seated at the table. There were several teenagers of various ages in the room. Offin pushed back his chair, supported his feet on the table in a relaxed pose, and commenced to hold forth on what he would do if he could influence the placement of light poles.

After several minutes Mrs Offin called from another room asking if anyone had seen her Drivers License, and most of those in the room replied "no". By this Offin had apparently assessed me by my youthful appearance as somewhat of a "rookie", as I parried his stupid comments. Then Mrs Offin re-entered the kitchen and said, "Lyall are you sure you haven't seen my license?"

"Narr.. forget it," he replied, as he prodded the table with an index finger, "Look my boy. I was driving the car, so what're you going to do about it?"

You bloody fool! (I thought)... what do you expect I'm going to do about it. I took out my notebook, recorded the current time and date, and asked what time the accident occurred. I wrote down his answer, then asked if he had had anything to drink since the accident. He cynically replied, "Yes I've had eighty-nine drinks!"

This was too much for Mrs Offin, she became angry and abused him. She said, "You drunken liar. He hasn't had anything to drink since the accident Constable. I knew this would happen. I told you you were too drunk to take the car out, but you wouldn't listen."

I told Mrs Offin that if her husband wanted to give me that answer that was his choice. Turning again to Offin I said, "Okay, so you say you have had eighty-nine drinks, what were they?

He then said that he hadn't drunk any liquor since reversing the car into the light pole. That was it. I told him I intended to arrest him and charge him with drunken driving, but I added that in view of the time lapse, and the fact that he was now in his own home, he could either agree to accompany me to the lock-up or I would obtain an arrest warrant.

Offin said I wouldn't need a warrant as he would come with me, but he wanted to telephone his solicitor before leaving. After quite some delay following Offin's call to his solicitor, as he had a shower and several cups of strong coffee, we left together in the Police car for Central Police Lock-up having arranged through Police Communications for other police to stand-by the fallen power lines.

I'll never forget the basic details of the conversation we had as we travelled to the lock-up. I was astonished by Offin's arrogance and his garrulous remarks. He started off by saying what a rotten state of affairs it was that a man (like him), who was only "trying to do the right thing", should end up being arrested by the police. I countered this by pointing out that he only had himself to blame as I too had been trying to do the right thing by him, yet he had tried to make a fool of me by challenging me to arrest him. He agreed and said he wouldn't have thought much of me as a man if I hadn't arrested him.

Then he dropped a bombshell! He said, "But I feel sorry for you as I am the Associate to the Chief Justice of the Supreme Court of Western Australia (he really was a Judge's Associate, but not to the Chief Justice). A gentleman held in highest esteem, and the Court is unlikely to believe the word of a mere police constable in preference to the word of a person of my standing."

Oh gawd!(I thought) ... he's probably right. I had little enough evidence in the first place, and now to be told this. But then, even if I had known who he was right from the start, I'm sure I wouldn't have handled it in any other way. Now I had a battle royal on my hands, but it didn't weaken my resolve. I said, "Well Mr Offin, if that's the way it turns out, so be it. But when we get to Court I'll be telling the truth. You can say whatever you like, but we'll both know that I've told the truth and that's all that matters. And I warn you now that whatever you say to me, I intend to repeat in Court as evidence."

It made no difference. He continued to babble on about how sorry he felt for policemen as he sat there listening to them giving evidence during a Criminal trial; how they were commonly attacked and accused of lying as a defence counsel tactic, that this was what I too could expect from his counsel when we got to court (how right he was). And as he kept up his chattering, I listened carefully and tried to make a mental note of all he said.

When we arrived at the lock-up, Mr Leo Wood, Offin's solicitor (a leading Criminal Lawyer) was waiting in the charge room with the Sergeant in charge, who was obviously intimidated by the presence of such eminent counsel, as he virtually let him take charge.

Remember, at that time, there was no breathalyser to support the police evidence. Almost everything hinged on the arresting Constable's evidence, supported where possible by any evidence the Charge Room Sergeant may be able to give about the condition of the accused and questions he asked of him at the lock-up.

However Mr Wood quickly put paid to any help I'd get from that quarter. He told the Sergeant that apart from giving personal details, Offin would not answer any questions or undergo any sobriety tests. And he requested that Offin be admitted to Bail forthwith, on his own surety. Of course Mr Wood was quite properly looking after the interests of his client, but I did think the Sergeant could at least have made a token effort and asked Offin himself instead of immediately complying with his solicitor's directions. So as it was I was completely on my own. There was little the Sergeant could say in Court about Offin's condition that would support my evidence.

When we finally got to Court, Offin was represented by a barrister Mr Hatfield, a leading Q.C., assisted by Mr Kakulas as his junior counsel. Six witnesses, including Mr Wood his advising solicitor, were called by the defence, and I was the only witness for the prosecution. The scales of justice were definitely weighed against me and I felt I had little chance of success.

However my personal credibility apparently became a major point in my favour. As a front-line policeman I had appeared many times as a prosecution witness in the Courts, and most magistrates knew me as a credible witness. So when the defence sought to make me out as a fool and a liar, it simply wasn't plausible, it was inconsistent with my past behaviour

I gave my evidence fully, including my initial doubts about who may have been driving and my reason for taking the line of action that I had. I also related much of Offin's garrulous conversation as we drove to the lock-up. Then as expected Mr Hatfield, in his cross-examination, vigorously attacked me and sought to discredit my evidence. I particularly recall one line of questioning he used in an attempt to embarrass me. It was probably his first cross-examination question.

"Constable, when the defendant told you he had had eighty-nine drinks since the accident, you didn't take him seriously did you?"

This was a loaded question, a bit like in a boxing match when you see the punch coming and try to deflect or avoid it. So I replied, "If you mean, did I believe him..."

He cut me off, "Constable I'm not asking if you believed him. I'm asking did you take him seriously – answer the question, Yes or No!"

I tried again, "If you mean believe..."

Again he cut me off, "Good lord! surely you know the meaning of the word serious! You did go to school didn't you? You did have some education didn't you? Did you take the defendant seriously when he said he had had eighty-nine drinks since the accident? ...It's a simple enough question. I want your answer, Yes or No."

He had me "on the ropes", that last stab about my education was a bit below the belt and it hurt, but I wasn't about to give in to his bullying. So, like in a boxing match, I appealed to the referee – the Magistrate. Contrary to what some lawyers would like to believe, they don't have control of the Court proceedings, that prerogative rests with the magistrate or presiding judge. Ignoring Mr Hatfield, I turned to the Magistrate and said, "Your worship, I can't answer the question with a simple yes or no. I ask you to allow me to answer it more fully in my own way."

The Magistrate (who could no doubt see my problem) agreed and told me to proceed. I then explained that when Offin told me he had had eighty-nine drinks since the accident, I didn't believe him, but I did take a serious view of the fact that he chose to answer such an important question in so frivolous a manner. I'd turned the tables on the Q.C. By answering his question as I did, I'd managed to re-emphasize the irrational conduct of his client. So he cross-examined me a little more cautiously after that.

When the defence witnesses were called, almost without exception they attempted to make me out as a fool, obsessed with the intention of arresting Offin for drunken driving, while ignoring the dangerous situation created by the fallen power lines. It's a wonder they didn't suggest I was frothing at the mouth. And, because they focused their attention on discrediting me, the police prosecutor was able to trip them up on several small but important points. It was a very harrowing ordeal for me, as the case dragged on (due to adjournments) for week after week. The media attention, because a Judge's Associate was involved, didn't help much either, as the more sensational aspects of the case were reported and highlighted in the daily press. The newspapers had a field day as some defence witnesses maliciously attacked me in Court, and my spirits sank lower and lower, it seemed so unfair. The Daily News newspaper even published a photo of me in uniform leaving the Court building, as part of their headline story about how a defence witness alleged I had behaved. Their headline (in block print) screamed "CONSTABLE ACTED LIKE IDIOT."

But while I was wilting under the stress of these attacks, it seems the credibility I had established with the presiding Magistrate carried far more weight than I realised. For, to my great relief and surprise, he finally ruled in my favour and convicted Offin as charged.

It had taken about four or five long months for the matter to be finalized. And for the case to have been won against such odds, was not only a true victory for justice but it also boosted my faith in that what I was doing (the way I carried out my duty) was right.

I was involved in a lot of defended matters during my time as a "front line" policeman, and later, but none caused me more stress or affected me more deeply than the drunk driving charge I preferred against Lyall Offin the Judge's Associate.

*   *   *   *   *

Describing the difficulties I had with Lyall Offin, and thinking about some of the other drunk driving charges I was involved in during my time on the Beat and in the Bush, causes me to to also recall the following humorous incident which occurred several years after I left Innaloo:

It was about 6.30pm one Friday evening in early December 1974 by the time my fellow Sergeant and workmate Brian and I cleared the outskirts of the city and headed for home, travelling North on Charles Street with the tail-end of the peak hour traffic. As members of the Commercial Agents Squad we had been working late in conference with the Crown Prosecutor, preparing for a District Court trial due to commence on the following Monday. I was driving the un-marked police car and we were both in plain-clothes. As was the practice, I was to drop Brian off in Yokine before heading home myself. I had been home late several times during the week and on leaving home that morning had promised to take my wife out to dinner – assuring her I would be home no later than 6pm, and here it was already after 6.30.

Then as we cleared the intersection of Vincent Street the dual lanes of north bound traffic slowed to a crawl. Clearly there was a major obstruction ahead and I assumed it was a traffic accident. "Damn," I muttered.

171

This was all we needed – a bloody traffic accident to hold us up (or so I thought from the way the traffic was moving). However as we crawled forward with other traffic approaching the intersection of Scarborough Beach Road Mount Hawthorne, I saw that the obstruction was a clapped-out old Ford ute, loaded with scaffolding planks and trestles. It was in the left lane slowing weaving left to right in the typical manner of a drunken driver. Overtaking cars were being forced to hold back until they had a chance to shoot past without risking a prang.

Although we were off duty and running late for home commitments, there was no question where our priority lay.

As we passed through the intersection of Scarborough Beach Road I pulled alongside the utility and Brian called on the driver to stop, identifying us as the police. The driver beamed a smile and gave us a salute acknowledging the order as he followed then stopped behind us at the kerb in Charles street just north of the intersection.

We walked back together to the utility and asked the driver to get out. A solidly built bloke aged about forty-five, he was dressed in a work-stained black singlet, football shorts and socks rolled down over heavy work-boots. The smell of stale beer on his breath combined with that of his soiled clothes and body odour made him seem about as rank as a billy-goat's backside. He was drunk alright, in fact he was almost leg-less as we helped him walk around his vehicle to the footpath on the other side. He was a "happy-go-lucky" sort of a cove, not the least bit aggro about being stopped. He said he was a "bricky's off-sider", and that after the building job he'd been on finished about mid-day he and the rest of the team had been "having a few" in the pub all afternoon. It was a simple straight-forward case of drunken driving, but for a number of reasons (not the least of which my personal arrangements) we really didn't want the hassle of getting further involved.

Additionally we didn't have an "Alco preliminary

breath test" kit in our vehicle (the approved preliminary breath testing equipment then in use). So I returned to our car and contacted Police communications on the radio. I advised the operator we were off duty, that we had stopped a suspected drunken driver and required a Traffic patrolman to attend and take over.

Within minutes a Traffic Patrol car pulled into the kerb and I walked forward to speak with the young patrolman – who was the sole occupant in the vehicle. Introducing myself I explained what had happened and that we were in a hurry.

I added, "Look. It's really quite straight-forward. As you'll see the bloke is done like a dinner. We'll give you our particulars and enough detail for the preliminary brief. If you need statements from us later that won't be a problem but we do have to get away as quickly as possible now."

"Oh please Serg.!" the young man almost pleaded, "Please don't leave me on my own with this. I've only been out of the (police) school about a week and this is the first time I've been out on patrol on my own. Although I've got the Alco breath test gear with me I've never used it in a real situation."

Oh great! I personally knew nothing about the use of preliminary breath test equipment or the procedure for taking a sample. Preliminary breath testing was not a factor when I last worked in the operational area and I didn't know whether my mate Brian knew much about it either. Never-the-less we could hardly leave the young probationer on his own. So gathered in a small group in front of our amiable drunk (who was now leaning back on the left front mudguard of his car to avoid falling over) we examined the gear and discussed how to put it together so it would operate.

As most operational policemen would know, use of the Alco Preliminary Breath Testing equipment is not very complex – providing the operator understands and follows the correct procedure. But at that time I hadn't even seen a damn preliminary breath test conducted.

Although Brian was not that confident, he took the lead role in fitting the gear together as the probationer and I offered advice on what we thought should be done. Our amiable suspect took a great interest in what we were doing and also put in a word or two himself – it was a bit like the blind leading the blind.

Suddenly our drunken friend stumbled forward almost knocking us off balance... "Ya silly buggers!" he said, "You're puttin' it on the wrong end! I've done this before. 'ere give me a bit-of-a-go will ya." As he spoke he snatched the bits and pieces from Brian and, with almost practised skill, fitted them in the correct order and inflated the bag with one huge breath.

Proud of his efforts, he held the bag up for us to see. And as we watched the level of green rise steadily past "the point of no return" indicating a positive test, I nearly choked controlling my laughter as, swaying on his feet, our drunken friend said, "Ya see! That's how it's done! I told ya I'd done it before."

He clearly WAS an expert.

*　　*　　*　　*　　*

Of course Probationary Constables can't always get such "expert" advice. When they first start out they often have to work alone without the help of a more experienced officer. So they do make mistakes and hopefully learn by the experience. The following small story provides a good example of this:

"He's gone Sarg! He's gone!"

There was a note of panic in the voice of the young probationary constable addressing me in the Muster-room at Central Police station. It was about 7pm one evening early in June 1982. I was the Senior Sergeant rostered as Officer in charge of the afternoon relief.

It was that time of the night when there was quite a movement of staff coming and going as they booked in for their evening meal break. City station had not yet opened and beat constables were transferred back and forth from the city centre by small shuttle-buses. As was quite common we were short of experienced staff. There was only one junior sergeant to assist me in the office, and most of the probationary constables who had graduated from the Academy the previous week had to work un-supervised, walking the beat on their own or in company with another probationer.

I was in the office on my own at the time (my second sergeant on meal break) trying to cope with the telephones and answer queries coming in from the beat constables on their hand held two-way radios, when I noticed a burst of activity in the Muster-room just outside my office. Everyone seemed to be either running or shouting.

I stepped from the office, raising my voice to make myself heard above the din. "What's going on?" I asked of the men rushing past. One of the probationers stopped to answer me – "He's gone! Sarg! He's gone!"

"Who's gone? Just settle down a minute and tell me what's going on."

"Our prisoner Sarg. Our prisoner's gone"

"What do you mean?"

The young man, Probationary Constable Simms (not his real name) aged about twenty, almost gabbled out his embarrassing story. It seems that he and another probationer of about the same age (Jones will do for his name) were on the beat in Murray Street Perth when the manager of a Menswear store drew their attention to a man he had seen take an item of underwear from the store, hide it under his shirt and leave without paying. The offender, who was pretty well under the weather, was stopped and searched by the constables. They found the stolen clothing on him and confirmed he had taken it without paying. So they arrested the man for shop stealing and brought him to Central Police Station. But instead of taking their prisoner straight to the lock-up, they brought him to the Muster-room as they wanted to check his details on the computer in case there were any outstanding warrants for him or if he was wanted for other matters.

Simms said, "We sat him on one of the forms over there. At first I stayed with him, but my mate was having trouble with the computer so I walked over to help him. It seemed okay as there must have been at least a half a dozen other blokes (police) in the room at the time. A minute or two later when I looked back he was gone. We're try'n to find him now but he doesn't seem to be in the building."

Oh great! (I thought) This is all I need. I had recently transferred back to Central Station from Training Branch. My anticipated promotion to Commissioned Officer (Inspector) was not far off. I needed a change and wanted to demonstrate that although I had been out of the General Duties operational area for some years I had not lost touch with front-line policing. Unfortunately under the rather draconian management practices then in place, the senior supervising officer was often held responsible for the errors of staff under their command. Never-the-less I put these thoughts behind me as my immediate priority was to co-ordinate the search to recover the escapee as quickly as possible.

I obtained a description of the man, issued a "Urgent Look-out To Be Kept for Escapee" message, and ordered all available police in the building to make a search of nearby streets and adjacent parkland. I also arranged for an unmarked car to call at the home address given by the prisoner. Then, with my spirits sinking lower as time went by and the escapee had not been found, I wrote the incident up in the station Occurrence Book, logging times and completed stages of the search. The return of my office sergeant from his meal break only added to my gloom when he mournfully endorsed my fears about the effect the escape of a prisoner could have on my imminent promotion.

About three quarters of an hour passed. No trace of our escapee had been found and it was time to scale down the search. I recalled the foot-patrols and directed all staff to resume their normal duties. The beat constables assembled in the Muster-room and were being progressively bussed back to the city area.

I checked the details of the event again with Probationary Constables Simms and Jones, told them to go back to their beat in the city and to come in at least an hour before the end of the shift to complete a full report.

Simms spoke up, "Sarg, would it be okay if we walked up town instead of taking the shuttle-bus. We know what the bloke looks like and we just might pick him up on the way?"

"Yeah sure", I answered dejectedly – at that point I could see my own career in tatters and there was damn little I could do about it.

They were gone less than a minute or two when they suddenly re-appeared at my door – a struggling man held firmly between them. "We got 'im Sarg! we got 'im!", they joyously cried almost in unison.

"Where in the hell was he?" I asked in disbelief.

"He was comin' in the front door!" one of them replied.

Coming in the front door… of the station. Oh Gawd! I thought, what in the blazes is going on?

Their prisoner, who did seem rather drunk, was still struggling and protesting about being man-handled and restrained. I signalled them to let him go and told the man to sit down. "Okay now where have you been?" I questioned. "You were under arrest and the Constables left you sitting in the room out there. You've been missing for almost an hour."

"I went over-t-the Ozone (Hotel) to buy me some smokes." he slurred.

"You what!"

"Yeah… Well these two coppers brought me in here for nothin', and they said "Sit down and wait". I needed a smoke. I said "Giv'us a smoke will ya" and they told me to shut up. I sat there dyin' for a smoke and asked some of the other coppers to give me one, but they wouldn't. So I walked 'round the room lookin' for a cigarette machine. There wasn't one so I went over-t-the Ozone an' bought a bloody packet. Yeah and I had a few drinks while I was there too. I was comin' back. Just walkin' in the front door when these bastards grabbed me. Nearly broke me bloody arms they did."

Oh... what a fiasco! Of course the man had technically "escaped from legal custody", but it probably wouldn't have happened if the probationers had been more experienced. They should not have been working alone and it was the first time they had ever arrested anyone. When I considered all of the circumstances I believed it was not appropriate to charge the man with escaping from custody or to take disciplinary action against the probationers. I told Simms and Jones to only charge their prisoner with the shop stealing offence for which he had been arrested and I firmly cautioned them to take greater care when they had a prisoner in custody. I also gave the bloke a stern warning about leaving the police station as he had, and the two young constables took him away to the lock-up for processing.

That should have been the end of it, but I had only just completed the write-off in the Occurrence Book when one of the Central Station "Duty Inspectors" arrived to make a routine check of the entries. The Inspector, an indecisive man, was astounded when he read how I had finalised the missing prisoner episode. He urged me (in my own interest) to reconsider my decision as he believed the prisoner should have been charged with escaping from custody and that the two probationers ought to be formally disciplined for neglect of duty.

Unfortunately the Inspector's attitude was typical of many mid-level managers in the Police Force at that time – who considered the "Big Stick" approach to be the most effective management tool. His main fear was what the "Ayatollah" (the nick-name of our autocratic Chief Superintendent) would do unless full disciplinary measures were applied. However although the Chief

Superintendent was a stern disciplinarian, I knew him as a fair officer who I thought would, when he became aware of the circumstances, fully support my decision.

I failed to convince the Inspector that nothing would be gained by "nailing the probationers to the wall" for a simple error of judgement, and that if the prisoner chose to defend the escaping from custody charge the Police would be made to look foolish. When he persisted I put him on the spot by asking him if he was, in effect, ordering me to submit a formal report on the incident when I had already finalised it as a marginal matter. I pointed out that my report would clearly state I was reporting under protest at his direction, and that I would recommend my actions be endorsed. That set him back a bit! As I suspected, he wasn't prepared to make such a direction, and he left my office still voicing his disapproval.

Unbeknown to either of us the two probationary constables, having lodged their prisoner in the lock-up, had been waiting in the Muster-room outside my office and apparently overheard the interchange between the Inspector and me. I can imagine how they felt as their fate seemed to be hanging in the balance.

After the Inspector left, they knocked on my door and asked if they could speak with me. I noted how apprehensive they looked. Jones spoke for them both, "Sorry Sarg, but we couldn't help over-hearing what the Inspector said. Do you think we could be charged?"

Poor kids. I could understand how they felt. Only out of training school a few days, and here they were worried about getting into serious trouble at such an early stage of their career.

"No." I said, with a little more confidence than I felt, as the Occurrence Book entries still had to survive scrutiny by the Ayatollah, "I'm sure the Chief Super-intendent will agree with my decision. The important thing is, have you learnt by the experience?"

"Yes. We sure have," they replied.

"Well," I continued, "it won't always be this simple.

When you do make a mistake accept it for what it is and move on. And if you're honest about it, you'll usually get the support of your senior officers. Now you'd better get back to your beat."

As they turned to go they both looked much relieved. Simms hesitated at the office door, "Gee thanks for stickin' up for us Sarg." he said. "We really thought we were gone when we heard what the Inspector said."

In the ongoing hub-bub of police service, I never came in contact with "Simms" or "Jones" again, but they're probably still out there somewhere continuing the good fight. And I'm fairly confident they have never forgotten the night their first prisoner went "absent without leave" to buy himself some smokes.

Oh yes, my assessment of the Ayatollah proved correct, as he never questioned my decision to finalize the matter as I did.

EPILOGUE

There are many levels and components to the Police Service. From the Commissioner and his other senior administrative officers down to recruit level, each member has an important contribution to make to the quality of service the public receives. And although the Service could not operate as effectively without the benefit of various specialised sections and branches, like Traffic and Criminal Investigation, none are more vital than the dedicated men and women, broadly referred to as "General Duties Police". These are the people who work at the "coal face" of the job, closest to the public, and who in most cases are the first on the scene when police are required. How these police personnel conduct themselves often becomes the standard by which the community judges the Service as a whole.

Because General Duties is the first operational level of the Service, the starting point of each officer's career, it is the area where a lot of sorting out takes place. Where inexperienced people like I was, find what the real world is really like; where they have to learn to cope with stress, and develop a good level of discipline so they can do the things they have to do. When they make an honest mistake, as they sometimes do, or find the going almost too hard to handle they have to be resilient; to bounce back, learn from the experience and get on with the job.

The anonymous sage who wrote the "Serenity Prayer", must have been thinking of policemen when he did so, for I believe it provides an excellent philosophy for police to live by. I know I have often asked... "God (to) grant me the serenity to accept the things I cannot change," – the situations, the tragedies I was unable to do anything about;..."with the courage to change the things I can" - I'm pretty sure that without His help in this area, I could not have achieved the things I did; and the tricky last one ... "and the wisdom to know the difference." – well with this it would be grand if we really could achieve such a level of wisdom (the important thing is to try). But the ghosts and the doubts will sometimes creep back. I guess that too is the legacy of police service.

Being a policeman is not a "fun" job – I have many sad memories that I'd like to forget – but it can at times be very rewarding. The trick seems to be that you must try not to become too cynical; to think positive and try to maintain a sense of humour.

In December 1968 an opportunity arose for me to transfer from Innaloo to a day-shift inquiry job at the Police Firearms Branch. So after more than 16 years "on the beat and in the bush" the General Duties chapter of my police service closed, and the door opened on a new phase of my career in various specialised sections and administrative areas of the Police Service.

THE COP

*No bard embalms the cop in song, few people praise or
toast him; whate're he does is always wrong so we unite to
roast him. He is the butt of hoary jests- canst name the time
he wasn't? We damn him if he makes arrests and damn him
if he doesn't. We cuss him daily for his sins, with criticisms
haunt him; for every peeler should be twins - he's never where
we want him. We blame him if some schoolboy hits our little
Willie; we blame him if the cat has fits or if the cow goes silly.
He guards the traffic in great style, from blockades and
congestions, and answers with a kindly smile five million
silly questions. When those who roast him daunted stand, in
times of strife and riot, he takes his life and club in hand and
scraps for peace and quiet. He hunts the bad man and the
yegg, he walks all night with dangers, and gets a bullet in
the leg pursuing deadly strangers. He seeks in dark and
noisome lairs the burglar who eschews him, and in our cosy
rocking chairs we sit up and abuse him.*

– Walt Mason
Extract from W.A. Police News, November 1956.

*...the needs of the community are best served when
police make intelligent use of their discretion and enforce
statutory laws as circumstances dictate.*

*...policemen ought to be seen essentially as peace officers
and conflict resolvers ... law enforcement although important,
ought not to be the prime objective.*

Extracts from - "An overview of the functions of the
Western Australian Police Force." August 1, 1984.

"When an old person dies, a library is lost."

- Tommy Swann